IMAGES
of Sport

MILLWALL
FOOTBALL CLUB
1940-2001

MILLWALL FOOTBALL CLUB

FOOTBALL LEAGUE DIVISION TWO

SATURDAY NOVEMBER 26th, 1966

v

CARLISLE UNITED

kick off 3.15 p.m.

OFFICIAL PROGRAMME   PRICE SIXPENCE

The programme cover for a record-breaking game against Carlisle. The Lions' 2-1 win meant that they had notched up 56 consecutive unbeaten League games, to surpass Reading's pre-war record.

IMAGES
of Sport

MILLWALL
FOOTBALL CLUB
1940-2001

Compiled by
Chris Bethell and David Sullivan
(on behalf of the Millwall FC Museum)

TEMPUS

Millwall FC, 1939/40. From left to right, inset: F.G. Weedon (vice chairman). Back row: C. Kennard (staff), McMillen, Williams, Beattie, Dudley, Walsh, J. Fort (staff). Fourth row: A. Bridges (staff), J. Anderson (staff), Chiverton, E. Smith, Jinks, Toser, Forsyth, Lea, Fenton, W. Moor (groundsman). Third row: W. Voisey (trainer), Fisher, Richardson, Osman, McLeod, Pearson, Burke, Yuill, Daniels, Sykes, Brolly, Bower, J. Collins (assistant trainer). Second row (seated): D.J.W. Conquest (assistant secretary), G.E.O. Max (director), P.R. Higson (director), C. Hewitt (manager), A.H. Gould (director), J. Beveridge (director), T. Thorne (chairman). Front row: Rawlings, Thorogood, J.R. Smith, Barker. Millwall played three games before the Football League was suspended because of the outbreak of the Second World War. The results of those three games were: 26 August v. Newcastle (h), 3-0 (Brolly, Richardson 2); 28 August v. Plymouth (h), 0-2; 2 September v. Bradford (a) 2-2 (Beattie, Richardson).

First published 2001
Reprinted 2002, 2004

Tempus Publishing Limited
The Mill, Brimscombe Port,
Stroud, Gloucestershire, GL5 2QG
www.tempus-publishing.com

© Millwall FC Museum, 2001

The right of Millwall FC Museum to be identified as the Author
of this work has been asserted in accordance with the
Copyrights, Designs and Patents Act 1988.

British Library Cataloguing in Publication Data.
A catalogue record for this book is available from the British Library.

ISBN 0 7524 2187 5

Typesetting and origination by Tempus Publishing Limited.
Printed in Great Britain.

Contents

Millwall FC Museum

At the present time, the Millwall FC Museum has no permanent home and has been putting on temporary exhibitions at local venues. This book has been compiled by Chris Bethell and David Sullivan, who have been keen Millwall supporters for many years and are part of the body of historians who are custodians for the proud heritage of Millwall Football Club, The Lions of London.

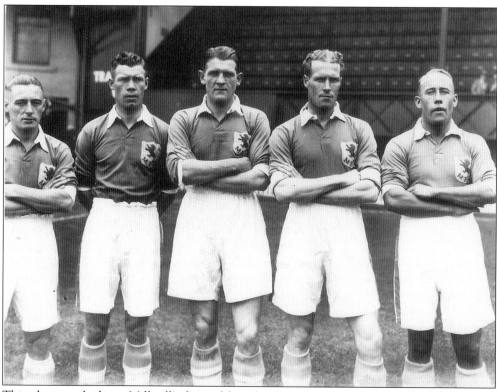

This photograph shows Millwall's forward line for the game at Bradford on the 2 September 1939, which preceded Britain's declaration of war against Nazi Germany. This was to be The Lions' last competitive Football League fixture for seven years, and the players featured here, from left to right, are: Freddie Fisher, Jimmy Richardson, Jimmy Beattie, Don Barker and Reg Smith. Fisher was a Yorkshireman, who was to lose his life in the Second World War whilst serving with the Royal Air Force. Geordie Jimmy Richardson would return to the club after the conflict, but his contribution would be minimal, as he was badly affected by the absence of regular competition. Centre forward Jimmy Beattie was a Scotsman who came to the club from Portsmouth during the summer of 1939, but would never play for Millwall in a recognised first team match. Don Barker came through the conflict unscathed, and would finish his career down at Brighton. Outside-left J.R. 'Reg' Smith would go on to carve out a livelihood in the game as a manager with Scottish clubs Dundee and Falkirk, before returning to The Den in 1959 to take over the managerial reins from Jimmy Seed. The game at Bradford ended 2-2, with Beattie and Richardson scoring.

Introduction

When the Second World War ended in 1945, Millwall faced the task of getting back to some sort of normality after nearly six years of deprivation. People who had survived the horrors of war were looking forward to the resumption of peacetime football, but for those who had followed The Lions before 1940, the immediate post-war period was to be one in which hope quickly turned to frustration and a lot of despair.

The second season after the war saw The Lions relegated, and the return of Charlie Hewitt – who replaced the unfortunate Jack Cock as manager – in the hope of restoring the club's fortunes. It was not to be. Apart from the 1952/53 season, when Millwall finished as runners-up to Bristol Rovers, and enjoyed a few high profile cup ties, Hewitt's second spell was far from pleasant and ended in his acrimonious sacking in 1956 (which was soured even further when he sued the club for wrongful dismissal).

Even during these desperate times, Millwall still had the players from whom the fans could expect maximum effort, such as Jimmy Constantine, Johnny Johnson, George Fisher, and Ronnie Mansfield. The hope for better things rested upon the emerging talents of Pat Saward, Malcolm Finlayson, and Charlie Hurley. Despite these stalwarts, however, the club went from one mediocre season to another throughout the 1950s, which all came to a head when Millwall became founder members of the new Fourth Division in 1958.

It took them four years to get promoted, and just two get demoted once more, but along the way the club produced another breed of player, with local lads like Joe Broadfoot and Dave Harper leading the way, their performances supplemented by the goals of Peter Burridge and Dave Jones. The foundation had been laid for success in the mid-1960s, when two consecutive promotions were achieved (in 1965 and 1966) under the man of the moment, manager Billy Gray, whose leadership gave the fans something to be proud of.

After the consecutive promotions, Millwall settled down to enjoy an unbroken run of eight seasons in the Second Division, with 1972 representing the nearest The Lions had been to achieving top-flight status for the first time. After the departures of the Billy Gray and Benny Fenton, the club appointed Gordon Jago as manager in late 1974. Although he brought an unlikely promotion in his first full year, his tenure also ended with unfulfilled dreams, and over the next five years another generation of Millwall supporters would suffer the same fate their predecessors had in the austere 1950s, with only the youth team bringing some joy to New Cross by winning the FA Youth Cup for the time, in 1979.

The making of the modern Millwall probably coincided with George Graham's arrival at The Den, when he steered the club back on an even keel – after they were apparently doomed to face the ignominy of Fourth Division football again. George had other ideas, and not only did The Lions avoid the drop, but they consolidated for another term, with the main prize coming in 1985 when he led his team to promotion as runners-up.

George had one more year at Cold Blow Lane, before setting off to his beloved Arsenal. He was replaced by another Scot, John Docherty, whose appointment didn't appear to be what the fans wanted. Their concerns seemed justified when his initial season saw Millwall struggle to garner enough points to survive. But although the Doc's first season had been unimpressive, a year further down road it was he who led Millwall into the promised land of First Division football by winning the Second Division, with Lions legends like Teddy Sheringham, Tony Cascarino, Terry Hurlock, and Les Briley leading the way.

Two campaigns in the top flight was all that Millwall could manage, and perhaps being a decent Division One (old Second Division) side was not such a bad thing, with Bruce Rioch attempting to build a footballing team that had the fans drooling one minute and pulling their hair out the next. But events on the pitch were becoming secondary concerns, as the club were now looking to expand after tasting the delights of big time football.

A new ground was being constructed at Senegal Fields – a 20,000 all-seater stadium and the first major ground to be built in London for over sixty years. This was seen as the first step to greater things, and so it appeared as the team reached the play-offs in the New Den's first season. It all came crashing down around the directors' ears, however, as The Lions lost both games against Derby, with major crowd trouble following the second match.

When Reg Burr retired as chairman, it was lifelong fan Peter Mead who took the reins of leadership, funding Mick McCarthy's forays into the transfer market during the close season of 1995. When Millwall, who were leading Division One at Christmas, signed two Russian internationals the following January, it appeared nothing could prevent The Lions from advancing into the Premiership. Once again The Lions were thwarted as the continued touting of McCarthy for the Irish national team manager's job finally became fact, and he was replaced by Jimmy Nicholl. No matter what Nicholl attempted to do, everything conspired against him, with Millwall going into free fall, not only down the division but eventually out of it, as relegation reared its ugly head once more. In less than a year Nicholl and his assistant Martin Harvey were relieved of their duties as the club found themselves in yet another financial straitjacket, and were forced into administration in January 1997

A new chairman, with new ideas and armed with a decent business plan, then took over; Theo Paphitis pledged that Millwall would get back to the higher reaches of football. He gave himself five years to achieve this goal, but it was managed in just four. Theo kept his word that the promising youngsters, like Neil Harris and Lucas Neill, wouldn't be sold off just for the sake of it – perhaps Millwall's appearance at Wembley in 1999 for the Auto Windscreens Trophy final served to justify this strategy.

Fortune favours the brave, and everyone connected with Millwall Football Club got their reward when The Lions won the Second Division Championship in 2001 by playing an entertaining – and at times scintillating – brand of football, with the emerging talents of Steven Reid, Tim Cahill and of course Neil 'Bomber' Harris coming to the fore.

David Sullivan

Acknowledgements

On behalf of Millwall FC Museum, the authors would like to thank the following individuals who have all been of great assistance in the compilation of this book:

Brian Tonks, Graham Tonks and David Webster, who have acted as official Millwall photographers over the past three decades; without their expertise, this book would not have been possible.

John French, Tom Green, Richard Lindsay, Bob McCree, Richard Smart and Ted Wilding, for the use of their vast collection of memorabilia.

Ex-Millwall players Ray Brand, Joe Broadfoot, Malcolm Finlayson, George Fisher and John Shepherd, for the loan of their personal photos.

Ann Borland, wife of the late Gordon Borland, Millwall FC secretary, and John Williams, a relative of Mickey Purser, a former Millwall FC chairman, for the use of their family mementos.

Special thanks go to all the supporters who have sent us photos and cuttings, thus supplementing the archives for this book, and the Millwall FC Museum. And to all at Tempus Publishing for their help in producing the two books.

One
War and Peace

Extensive damage to The Den after a German air raid can be seen in the clear light of day, but it's a case of all hands to the pump as members of the groundstaff and volunteers begin to clear the playing surface after the Luftwaffe's handiwork. On the extreme right of the picture is head groundsman Bill Moor, who followed his father Elijah into the job. The Moor family's association with Millwall was continuous from when Elijah was first employed in 1886, right up until his son Bill finally called it a day sometime in the late 1950s. Bill Moor was given a well-earned benefit match, when Glasgow Celtic visited Cold Blow Lane in 1948, which Millwall won 3-2, in what was describe as a stormy game.

This photograph illustrates the old wooden tip-up seats that were situated in the old Main Stand, which was destroyed by fire in April 1943. Sitting in the front row, on the right, is John 'Tiny' Joyce, the former Millwall goalkeeper from the club's days on the Isle of Dogs. 'Tiny' was a member of Civil Defence during the Second World War.

This panoramic view of The Den was taken on the 18 March 1944, when Aldershot were the visitors, on Millwall's return to Cold Blow Lane. One can see the bomb-damaged terrace, and a very distressed looking clock. A bomb had fallen around Easter the previous year, and rendered that part of the ground unsafe. In this game there were two future England managers

These three fellows, Bill Moor (left), Billy Voisey (centre), and John Joyce, all saw lengthy service with Millwall. Moor was the assistant groundsman at The Den to his father, before taking over the head job when Elijah retired. Voisey had joined the club when they were still based on the Island in 1908, and his playing career with The Lions saw him appear in both the Southern and Football Leagues, either side of the First World War (in which Bill became a highly decorated combatant). 'Tiny' came from Burton-upon-Trent, first appearing in Millwall's goal as far back as 1900, when he made his debut in a 3-0 win over Spurs. He had a season with Blackburn Rovers in 1902/03, and in the course of his career John would sign for Millwall on three occasions, the last being in 1916 when he rejoined from Tottenham Hotspur. He was nearly forty years old when he played his last game for the club, and for twenty years thereafter he was the assistant trainer at The Den; he and Dick Jones took charge of the team affairs when Bob Hunter passed away in 1933.

of the 1970s on view: assisting Millwall was Ron Greenwood, and for Aldershot – which as an Army town probably had its best ever team at this time – was Joe Mercer, who would create a very entertaining England side in his spell as the national coach. A crowd of around 10,000 saw The Lions lose 0-5 in this Football League South Cup group match.

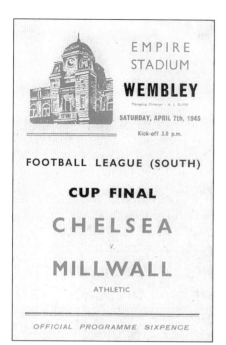

Programme cover from The Lions' first appearance at Wembley stadium. After playing well in the rounds leading to the final, they somehow managed to lose 2-0 to Chelsea – much like in a more recent game there when they went down 1-0 to an injury-time goal from Wigan Athletic in the Auto Windscreen Shield final in 1999.

HRH King George VI being presented to the Millwall team on their first ever appearance at Wembley, for the Football League South Cup final on 7 April 1945, where The Lions met their London neighbours Chelsea, who won 2-0. The player seen shaking hands with the King is Syd Rawlings, who came to Millwall in 1937, and on Syd's right is Len Tyler, another home-grown product who was born in Rotherhithe, but brought up and schooled on the Isle of Dogs. Len had also found time to supplement his income from football with earnings from work he achieved by becoming a part-time actor in the motion picture industry. The other players in this shot include goalkeeper Sam Bartram, whose own club Charlton Athletic would contest the first two post-war FA Cup finals; George Ludford of Spurs, another guest player; and two of Millwall's very own: Jimmy Jinks, who had made his League debut before the war, and Tommy Brown, who was regarded as the typical Scottish inside forward, who by all accounts could 'kill' a football no matter how hard it was played to him.

This terrific action shot from the Millwall *v.* Chelsea final clearly shows the famous twin towers. Unfortunately, The Lions didn't perform particularly well on the day, but they are pictured giving the 'Pensioners' a worrying moment as the Chelsea 'keeper Black appears to have lost his bearings – sadly, Millwall players Tyler, Jinks, T. Brown, and Rawlings could not take advantage of this. With the war in Europe now in its last days, there was a relaxation on the number of spectators allowed to attend games, and 90,000 people were in attendance for this match – certainly the largest crowd Millwall had ever played in front of.

Millwall FC, Football League South Cup final side, 1945. From left to right, back row: Bill Moor (groundsman), R. Phillips, R. Dudley, G. Fisher, E. Smith, S. Bartram, T. Brown, W. Voisey, A.S. Williams, J. Shaw, Jack Cock (manager). Front row: S. Rawlings, A. Brown, G. Ludford, J. Jinks, L. Tyler, G. Carney (trainer). Due to a colour clash, Millwall were required to change their strip. Unfortunately, having no spare kit, The Lions had to don an England strip, with a single lion badge sewn on over one containing three lions.

A day at the races during the 1944/45 season. From left to right, standing: W. Moor, G. Ross, E. Toser, M. Tilling, G. Duke, J. Richardson, S. Rawlings, J. Fisher, G. Hardy, H. Francis, D. Barker, J. O'Kambach. Kneeling: G. Dunkley, C. Bumstead, J. Hutton, A. Gregson.

This photograph shows the Millwall defence being stretched in the Football League South fixture against Brentford at The Den on the 22 December 1945. Doing their stuff for The Lions are: Reg Dudley (2), another player from the pre-war days who, before turning professional, won a England amateur cap in 1935; goalkeeper Charlie Bumstead, a south Londoner who also played for Crystal Palace and would return to The Den to coach the junior team in 1964; and George Fisher (on the ground), one of the most accomplished footballers ever to don a Millwall shirt. The 1946/46 season was to be the last season of regional wartime football, and Millwall won this particular game 3-1, with goals from Willie Hurrell, John Paton, and Johnny Johnson.

14

Benny Fenton was one of many players whose career was affected by the Second World War. He was signed by The Lions not long before hostilities broke out, joining the club from West Ham United in March 1939. An inside forward who would sometimes appear at half-back, Fenton assisted various clubs during the war years, and one of these was Millwall's neighbour, Charlton Athletic, who saw enough of Benny to fork out a fee of £6,000 to acquire his transfer in early 1947. Unfortunately for him, he had already played for Millwall in the FA Cup that season, and was thus deprived of a start in Charlton's cup-winning line-up later that year. Sadly, Benny passed away in the summer of 2000.

Stocky outside left Ronnie Mansfield saw wartime service with Royal Navy and was signed in 1942, just before being called up. He was involved in the Normandy landings, and later served with the Pacific Fleet. Returning to The Den in 1946, Ronnie became a regular in the Millwall first team. Although short in stature, he was very useful with his head, and in January 1950 he was awarded a long service cheque of £750. After appearing in 101 League and cup games for The Lions, Ron was transferred to Southend United in November 1952.

A crowd of some 38,000 spectators at The Valley in April 1946 witness Charlton and Millwall share the spoils in a 2-2 draw. This photograph shows Turner about to score the first Charlton goal, with Bumstead (goalkeeper) and Fisher the frantic Lions attempting to clear their lines.

For the first time in seven years the FA Cup was back, much to the delight of the football-watching public. For this season, 1945/46, a new format was used for the first time – it would later become a regular feature in the Football League Cup in the late 1970s – a two-legged tie for the early rounds. After defeating Northampton Town 5-2 on aggregate in the first round, Millwall were paired with mighty Aston Villa in the second. The first match at The Den resulted in a 4-2 win for the Midland team, with Jimmy Jinks scoring both the Millwall goals; this result made the second leg at Villa Park a mere formality, and so it turned out as Villa ran up a humiliating 9-1 reverse upon a stricken Millwall side. This picture shows Millwall's Irish international Tommy Brolly tackling Villa's winger Goffin at The Den in the first game.

Millwall players gather round 'keeper George Dunkley, whose leg was broken during a collison with Arsenal right winger Dr K. Flannagan. The doctor gave immediate medical attention during the match, which was played at White Hart Lane on 30 March 1946.

Millwall FC, 1946/47. From left to right, back row: L. Tyler, G. Bradley, R. Kelly, Middle row: C. Linney (secretary), G. Green (trainer), W. McMillen, J. Purdie, J. Jinks, J. Cock (manager), W. Voisey. Front row: J. Johnson, W. Hurrell, V. Woodward, T. Brolly, T. Brown, H. Osman. In this first full season after the Second World War, Millwall finished eighteenth in the Second Division, winning 14, drawing 8 and losing 20 of their games; they scored 56 goals and conceded 79. Johnny Johnson was the top scorer with 10 goals.

Down the years Millwall have occasionally had to live with a section of unruly fans, with warning notices being posted around The Den on quite a few occasions. At times this has blighted the club's progress, and in the first competitive Football League campaign after the war, Millwall were forced to play their 'home' match against Newcastle United at Selhurst Park, the ground of rivals Crystal Palace, on 13 December 1947. The novelty of this event attracted The Lions' biggest home attendance of the season, 33,362, which saw them win 2-1, with an own goal and one from Willie Hurrell, seen here having an attempt on the Magpies goal. Millwall would win only three more home fixtures during the remainder of the season, which ended in relegation – with many Millwall fans no doubt concurring that it was a pity the team could not have played the rest of the games at Selhurst!

Tottenham Hotspur v. Millwall, Easter Monday 29 March 1948. This was a depressing season for The Lions, and this match was the third over a holiday period which would yield just one point from a 0-0 Good Friday encounter with Spurs. This photograph was taken during the return game at White Hart Lane, and shows Millwall on the defensive, with Scottish 'keeper Malcolm Finlayson – who went on to win an FA Cup winner's medal with Wolves in 1958 – attempting to thwart a Spurs attack. He is being watched by the other Millwall defenders, who are Irishman Tom Brolly (left), and Welsh full-back Taffy Evans. After trailing 2-0 at the interval, The Lions pulled back two goals through Chris Simmonds and Willie Hurrell, only to go down 2-3. It would be another twenty-nine years before Millwall's next League match with Tottenham.

Millwall FC, 1947/48. From left to right, back row: R. Mansfield, J. Johnson, J. O'Kambach, R. Slade, C. Davies, V. Woodward. Middle row: T. Brown, G. Hardy, C. Simmonds, J. Purdie, J. Fisher, W. Morton, E. Smith, J. Jinks. Front row: J. Evans, R. Kelly, M. Tilling, W. Anderson, J. Cock (manager), G. Bradley, T. Brolly, R. Elliot, H. Osman. The picture was taken before a Blues v. Reds trial game at the beginning of the season. Millwall finished twenty-second, having won 9 games, drawn 11 and lost 22; they scored 44 goals and conceded 74. The top scorer was Willie Hurrell with 7 goals. The club was relegated to the Third Division (South).

Millwall FC, 1947/48. From left to right, back row: W. Voisey, C. Davies, G. Bradley, J. Purdie, J. Fisher, T. Brown, L. Tyler. Front row: J. Johnson, C. Simmonds, J. Jinks, J. Cock (manager), V. Woodward, R. Mansfield, W. McMillen.

Millwall FC, 1948/49. From left to right, back row: G. Fisher, S. Hobbins, R. Mansfield, C. Davies, J. Johnson. Middle row: T. Brolly, L. Tyler, C. Simmonds, F. Reeves, W. McMillen. Front row: L. Jones, W. Hurrell. Millwall finished eighth in the Third Division (South), winning 17 matches, drawing 11 and losing 14; they scored 63 goals and conceded 64. The top scorer was Jimmy Constantine with 23 goals.

The new season is nearly upon us and it's time for the annual Blues *v.* Reds public trial match. In this 1948 encounter, which was the curtain-raiser to Millwall's campaign back in Third Division, the players shown are, from left to right: Joe O'Kambach, Chris Simmonds, Mick Morton, Bob Gordon, and (defending his near post) full-back Len Tyler. This fixture would continue to be played on regular basis right up until the early 1960s. Usually, almost every member of the playing staff would get a run out during the match. Following the abolition of the maximum wage, the playing staff at the club became smaller and this type of fixture ceased. With the introduction of substitutes in 1965 and the gradual increase of players required on match days (five are now allowed on the bench), however, there may come a time when these games might be reintroduced.

An excellent crowd of 45,642, Millwall's biggest of the season, watches The Lions take on much-fancied Notts County in what was the division's match of the day. Featuring in the visitors' attack was none other than Tommy Lawton, the England international who County had signed from Chelsea to boost their promotion hopes, and he is shown here being tackled by Millwall's centre half Walter McMillen. It was, however, Millwall's centre forward, Jimmy Constantine, who stole the honours on that day – 23 October 1948 – with two cracking goals that gave The Lions a 3-2 victory. Constantine would score a total of 23 goals that season, including one hat-trick against Bristol City. Furthermore, Millwall went on to complete the 'double' over County by winning 3-1 at Meadow Lane the following March.

Millwall's new coach, Sam Weaver, had taken over from another former Newcastle United player, Jesse Carver, in the summer of 1949; Carver had taken a coaching job with Juventus and Weaver was brought in by Charlie Hewitt to take over. Sam was a noted wing-half in his playing days, having played at the highest level with Chelsea and Newcastle before the war and gained 3 England caps whilst with the Geordies. He was also a noted cricketer, playing for both Somerset and his native county, Derbyshire. Recruited from Leeds United, his first season at The Den was something of a disaster all round as Millwall had to seek re-election. Weaver was known for his long throw-ins and is pictured demonstrating this skill to a pair of Millwall players – Bradley and Myers.

Frank Hodgetts was signed in a much-heralded transfer in the close season of 1949 for £10,000 from West Bromwich Albion. His first season at The Den was something of a struggle, and after playing in 22 games in his initial season, Frank became more of a fringe first team player, and would appear in just another 14 League games over the next three seasons. Hodgetts is pictured taking on a Palace defender in the 1-1 draw at Selhurst Park on 20 January 1951, in a game in which he scored one of his 6 League goals for Millwall.

A rare meeting between the Arsenal and Millwall. This action comes from a first round tie of the London Challenge Cup in October 1949, which was played at Highbury. The Millwall players shown in this shot (where they appeared to have conceded a goal to the Gunners) are Des Quinn (2) – whose grandson, Rory Allen, would also become a professional footballer in the 1990s – Kenny Hencher (looking back), prostate goalkeeper Ted Hinton and onlooker Tom Brolly, all hailed from Northern Ireland. Millwall went on to win this match 3-2, with two goals from Len Townsend and one from Chris Simmonds. Unfortunately, The Lions bowed out in the next round a couple of weeks later, when Chelsea won 3-1 at The Den.

Two
The 1950s

Millwall FC, 1950/51. From left to right, back row: C. Hewitt (manager), A. Jardine, G. Fisher, J. Short, E. Hinton, F. Reeves, D. Quinn, S. Weaver (trainer). Front row: J. Johnson, J. Constantine, F. Neary, G. Bowler, S. Morgan, J. Hartburn. Millwall finished the season in fifth position, winning 23 matches, drawing 10 and losing 13; they scored 80 goals and conceded 57. The top goalscorer again was Jimmy Constantine with 26.

Millwall met Crystal Palace three times during the 1950/51 season (two wins and a draw). This action shot was taken during the FA Cup first round tie at Selhurst Park, which saw Millwall ease past their South-East London rivals 4-1, with goals from Johnson, Morgan, Neary, and Constantine – who is seen here challenging ex-Lion Charlie Bumstead, the Palace 'keeper, and centre half Watson. The Lions would go on to reach the fourth round of the competition; after beating Palace they defeated Bradford after a replay (1-0) and won a seven-goal thriller at Queen's Park Rangers in the third round, before another West London club, Fulham, halted their progress with a fortunate 1-0 win at The Den in front of 42,170 spectators.

Crosbie, the Bradford centre forward, beats Millwall 'keeper Ted Hinton to score past Jardine and the diving George Fisher. The game finished 1-1, and Millwall won the second round FA Cup replay at Bradford in December 1951 with the only goal of the game.

Malcolm Finlayson is out cold during a FA Cup third round game against QPR in January 1951. George Fisher (left) and Gerry Bowler are the players making their way to the crestfallen 'keeper. A crowd of 25,777 watched this match at Loftus Road, which Millwall won 4-3.

Millwall FC, 1951/52. From left to right, back row: R. Summersby, R. Brand, S. Anslow, P. Saward, R. Mansfield, A. Thrippleton, A. Monkhouse, A. White, W. Voisey. Middle row (players only): D. Quinn, A. Lyons, S. Weaver (trainer). Front row: E. Hinton, A. Jardine, J. Short, F. Reeves, G. Fisher, J. Johnson, J. Constantine, F. Neary, S. Morgan, J. Hartburn. This side finished fourth in the Third Division (South), winning 23 games, drawing 12 and losing 11, with 74 goals for and 53 against. The leading scorer was Frank Neary with 14 goals.

On your marks! Trainer and former pre-war Lion Jimmy Wallbanks puts Ron Mansfield and an unidentifieed team-mate through their paces during a training session at The Den. Jimmy was also a qualified physiotherapist, and was a former Lions player before the Second World War. Ron was a sturdy and forceful outside left, while Pat Saward was Millwall's first player to be capped by the Republic of Ireland, in March 1954.

To while away the time on long and tedious train journeys, footballers down the years have often relied on a pack of cards to enliven the many treks around the country, and the Millwall players shown here are no exception. Hoping no doubt to pick up a few quid from their colleagues in this particular game are Jimmy Constantine and Stan Morgan (both facing the camera), while Frank Reeves (looking back) has been momentarily distracted from his game, with George Fisher deep in concentration looking at his hand. The interested onlookers are, from left to right: Sam Weaver (trainer), Malcolm Finlayson, Des Quinn, and Johnny Short (all standing) with Frank Neary (sitting).

Millwall FC, 1952/53. From left to right, back row: J. Short, J. Shepherd, F. Reeves, G. Fisher, A. Thrippleton, F. Neary, P. Saward. Front row: A. Jardine, R. Mansfield, G. Stobbart, G. Bowler. J. Johnson, J. Hartburn, A. Monkhouse. The Lions finished second in the Third Division (South), winning 24 games, drawing 14 and losing 8; they scored 82 goals and conceded 44. Top goalscorer was John Shepherd with 15.

John Shepherd heads into the net for the first of his hat-trick against Barrow in a second round
FA Cup replay.

Alan Monkhouse heads towards goal with Shepherd (centre) while Stan Morgan looks on,
during this game at The Den. The Lions won 4-1, to go through to meet Manchester United in
round three.

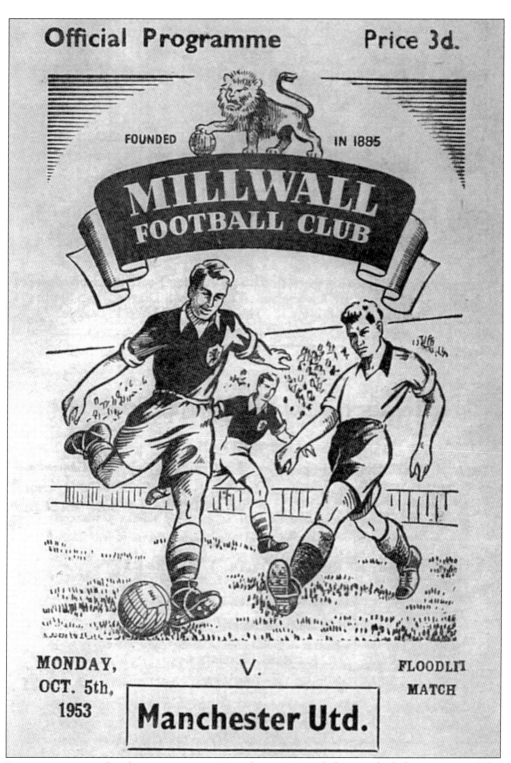

Official Programme Price 3d.

FOUNDED IN 1885

MILLWALL FOOTBALL CLUB

MONDAY, V. **FLOODLIT**
OCT. 5th, **MATCH**
1953

Manchester Utd.

Programme cover for the game against Manchester United that marked the opening of the floodlights. Over 20,000 were in attendance to see The Lions win 2-1.

The stylish Gerry Bowler turns the ball away from United's forwards in this 1953 FA Cup game, in which United took the tie with a goal late in the second half.

Taking a trot in the snow at The Den are, from left to right: Jardine, Saward, Shepherd, Johnson, Short, Hartburn, G. Fisher. This training was part of the preparation for the FA Cup match against Manchester United.

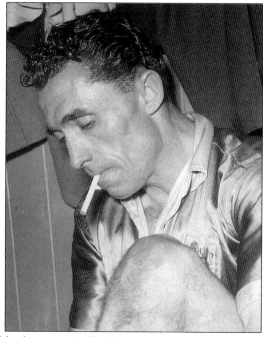

Left: Probably the finest post-war pairing of full-backs seen at Millwall were Scotsman Alex Jardine (leap-frogging) and George Fisher, pictured here during a training session at The Den. This splendid pair of footballers between them played in 650 games for The Lions and shared 31 goals (Jardine 334 games, 27 goals and Fisher 316 games, 4 goals). George, who was born where Millwall's current ground now stands, joined his boyhood club in the 1942/43 season, after being spotted by former Millwall player Bill Voisey. George, who was one of identical twins, would carve out a memorable career with The Lions; unfortunately his brother, Jack, who was also a full-back would play in just 3 Football League matches. After four years of serving in the Royal Air Force, for whom he appeared in representative games, George Fisher was a member of the Millwall team that reached Wembley in 1945. He turned into very reliable left-back as his career blossomed, and on occasions he would appear at outside left. He joined Second Division Fulham in 1954 and after a short stay at Craven Cottage went to Colchester, after linking up with former Lion, Benny Fenton, who was player-manager at Layer Road. Had Alex Jardine been playing for a more fashionable club, he might well have been selected for his country. Jardine was recruited from Dundee United in 1950 for a fee of around £700, and what a bargain he turned out to be. A solid and dependable defender, Alex, like Fisher, would appear on The Lions' right wing in some matches, and became the team's penalty taker. Injuries played a major role in his Den career, and after missing some games during the 1956/57 campaign, he picked up an Achilles tendon injury in 1958 that signalled the end of a marvellous career. He represented the Third Division (South) versus the North three times and also had three benefit games whilst at Cold Blow Lane. *Right*: A scene more reminiscent of a Sunday football dressing room, shows Frank 'The Brown Bomber' Neary smoking a cigarette, probably prior to the start of a benefit match – surely no manager would have allowed this to happen before a 'proper' game. Frank possessed an awesome shot from any distance and from any angle and was a real battler. It was these qualities that endeared him to the Millwall faithful. He first appeared for Fulham during the war, but was transferred to QPR at the start of the transitional season of 1945/46. There followed a move across London to West Ham for £4,000, but surprisingly the Hammers allowed him to leave for Leyton Orient after scoring 15 goals in 17 games. Millwall manager Charlie Hewitt, who had signed Neary for the O's back in October 1947, engaged Frank once again in August 1950 for a sum of £6,000. The first post-war player to score on both his Football League and FA Cup debuts for The Lions, in his four seasons at Millwall Frank would score 49 goals in 123 League appearances.

Millwall FC, 1953/54. From left to right, back row: P. Saward, G. Bowler, G. Fisher, A. Brewer, J. Shepherd, J. Heydon, J. Short. Front row: S. Weaver (trainer), G. Hazlett, G. Stobbart, F. Neary, F.A. Smith, J. Hartburn, A. Jardine. Millwall finished twelfth, winning 19 games, drawing 9 and losing 18; they scored 74 goals and conceded 77. George Stobbart was top scorer with 17 goals.

The view from the halfway line down the old railway track at Illderton Road, which also shows the tote board at the dog track and the original floodlights erected in 1953.

Charlie Hurley, Millwall's young centre half, was discovered by Bill Viosey when playing for Rainham Youth Club. Signed in October 1953, he made 110 appearances before joining Sunderland in September 1957, where he made over 400 appearances for the Rokerites. He went on to play for Bolton Wanderers in June 1969. Charlie gained the first of many caps when he played for the Republic of Ireland against England in May 1957.

Millwall FC, 1954/55. From left to right, back row: G. Fisher, J. Summers, J. Shepherd, D. Quinn, J. Short, M. Finlayson. Front row: G. Prior, S. Anslow, P. Saward, D. Pacey.

Millwall players Tony Brewer, John Shepherd, Stan Anslow and Ray Brand are seen giving assistant groundsman Fred Green a lift during a break in training.

Manager Ron Gray makes the players leap about at Deptford Park.

Ray Brand, a long serving centre half who waited four years for a first team place, competed with Charlie Hurley for the number five shirt. Brand could also play up front when needed and in over six seasons with the club he played 166 games and scored 8 goals.

A break from training and a pose for the cameras. From left to right: Malcolm Finlayson, Joe Tyrell, Stan Anslow, Johnny Shepherd, Ray Brand, George Prior and the young reserve player, Ben Jones.

Millwall FC, 1955/56. From left to right, back row: A. Jardine, J. Summers, A. Brewer, R. Brand, J. Smith, G. Veitch. Front row: G. Hazlett, J. Shepherd, C. Rawson, J. Tyrell, G. Prior. Millwall finished the season in twenty-second position, winning 15 games, drawing 6 and losing 25; they scored 83 goals and conceded 100. The leading scorer was again John Summers, who managed 24 goals.

An ex-Millwall XI turn out for John Short's testimonial. From left to right, back row: W. Moor, J. Short, S. Bartram, D. Quinn, F. Reeves, S. Morgan, F. Neary. Front row: F. Hartburn, R. Mansfield, W. Hurrell, G. Fisher, G. Bowler. The game, which was played on 12 March 1956, ended All Star XI 3, Ex-Millwall XI 4. The scorers for the Ex-Millwall XI were Neary, Hurrell, Reeves and an own goal.

Johnny Summers, Ken Hencher and John Shepherd pose outside the ticket office.

Millwall FC, 1956/57. From left to right, back row: A. Jardine, G. Veitch, W. Lloyd, C. Rawson, J. Smith, R. Brand. Front row: G. Hazlett, J. Shepherd, S. Anslow, D. Pacey, R. Summersby. Millwall finished seventeenth, winning 16 matches, drawing 12 and losing 18; they scored 64 goals and conceded 84. The leading scorer was John Shepherd with 17 goals.

Action from a game against Shrewsbury at the start of the 1956/57 season. George Veitch is heading away a corner, with goalkeeper Tony Brewer keeping an eye on the situation. John Smith and Alex Jardine are the players covering the goal-line just in case.

The programme cover for the FA Cup fourth round game against Newcastle on 26 January 1957 – Millwall's most famous post-war giant-killing feat.

Every inch of space was taken up when 45,646 crammed in to the Den to see The Lions take on the mighty Newcastle. The attendance of over 45,000 brought about a ground limit of 42,000 for subsequent high profile games. The last time this capacity had been reached was in a cup tie with Spurs in 1967 – which had been before other limitations were imposed, such as segregation of home and away fans and ground safety rules.

Bill Lloyd dives to push a low shot round the post, while left-back John Smith stands guard on the goal-line in the match against Newcastle. This victory was one of Millwall's best ever, considering Newcastle's record in the FA Cup during this period.

Celebrations in the bath after the FA Cup fourth round victory over Newcastle.

John Shepherd and Ray Brand sign autographs for two youngsters with 'keeper Tony Brewer looking on.

Mid-air duel between Shepherd and Birmingham 'keeper Merrick during the FA Cup fifth round match in 1957.

John Shepherd was known as a hat-trick specialist, and scored 82 goals in 172 appearances between 1952 and 1958. The club's top goalscorer in 1952/53 and 1956/57, his best return from a match was the four goals he scored on his debut against Leyton Orient in October 1952. Shepherd was the club's leading scorer in FA Cup ties, with 15 goals in 17 games. He eventually moved on to Brighton for two seasons before transferring to Gillingham, where he scored 21 goals in 53 League games.

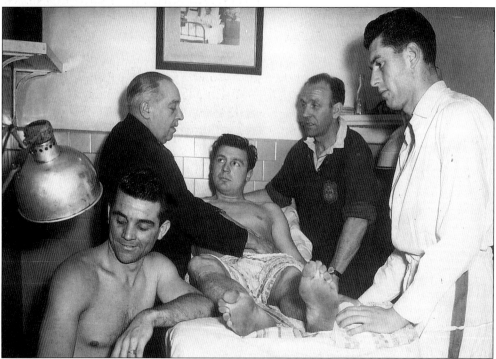

John Shepherd listens to Dr Eppel's diagnosis in the treatment room while Stan Anslow has a bit of shoulder treatment from the heat lamp. Trainer John Short and Ray Brand (*right*) await their turn.

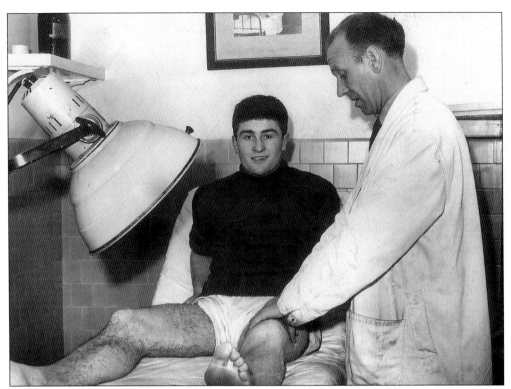

Charlie Hurley receives treatment from John Short. Hurley's career at The Den was disrupted by injury, and it certainly played a part in delaying his debut on the international stage for the Republic of Ireland.

London born Johnny Summers started with Fulham Juniors in 1947 and moved to Norwich City in 1950, before joining Millwall in May 1954. A favourite with the crowds, he made some spectacular strikes and was prolific with both feet, managing 43 goals in 97 appearances. Summers was transferred to Charlton in November 1956 and died in 1962 after a long illness.

Millwall FC, 1957/58. From left to right, back row: J. Short (trainer), S. Anslow, G. Veitch, C. Hurley, W. Lloyd, R. Brand, C. Rawson, J. Smith, R. Gray (manager). Front row: G. Hazlett, P. Hayes, J. Shepherd, D. Pacey, J. Roche, G. Pulley, R. Summersby. This side finished twenty-third in the last season of the Third Division (South), winning 11 games, drawing 9 and losing 26; they scored 63 goals and conceded 91. The top scorer was John Shepherd with 11 goals.

Terry Hall (an Oldham Athletic fan) was a popular ventriloquist during the late 1950s, whose main attraction during his many TV exposures, and the variety shows he appeared in up and down the country, was 'Lenny the Lion'. This publicity shot, taken at The Den sometime during the 1957/58 season, captures Terry and 'Lenny' with fellow Lions, Johnny Shepherd (left), Ray Brady and Ray Brand. Full-back Ray Brady, who signed for Millwall in 1957, was a player whose career took a turn for the better when he took up his position in the centre of the defence, and he became a rugged and formidable centre half who was joined by his brother, Pat, at Cold Blow Lane a year or so later. Ray Brand was a fine club man who served Millwall for a decade from 1951 until 1961, although he did not make his debut until the last day of 1955, when The Lions earned a point from a 2-2 draw at Crystal Palace. Normally a centre-back, on occasions Brand would be used as a temporary striker, and he scored some vital goals from that position. Between them, the three Lionhearts pictured here appeared in over 460 League games for the club.

Millwall FC, 1958/59. From left to right, back row: J. Seed (manager), C.F. Linney (secretary), G.S. Kenure (director), F.C. Purser (chairman), C. Rawson, R. Humphries, R. Brady, E. Jackson, K. Troup, R. Davies, R. Brand, H. Dove, D. Harper, H. Redmond, N. Weedon (director), Dr D. Eppel (director), J. Short (trainer), S.C. Hedge (director), S. Tickeridge (assistant trainer). Middle row: J. Roche, D. Bumpstead, D. Pacey, S. Anslow, C. Hazell, P. Hayes, R. Heckman, A. Crowshaw, L. Vaessen (kneeling in ordinary clothes). Front row: R. Summersby, J. Broadfoot, J.A. Miller, W. Craig, J. Howells. Millwall finished ninth in the newly formed Fourth Division, winning 20 games, drawing 10 and losing 16; they scored 76 goals and conceded 69. Ron Heckman top scored with 11.

One of the many players to be converted with great success from inside forward to half-back was Dave Bumpstead who, like his famous predecessor, the late Benny Fenton, was a product of Essex football. A native of Wennington near Rainham, Bumpstead first came to the fore with a works team, Briggs Sports. He later joined Tooting & Mitcham United, where his displays brought him to the attention of England selectors at amateur level and (like a Millwall contemporary of his, Ron Heckman) Dave would appear for his country before turning professional in 1957. A volatile and, at times, temperamental footballer, Dave did have his problems with the authorities, but his failings were far outweighed by his good points. On his day, his foraging midfield displays frequently saw him accurately spraying the ball to a colleague in space or putting his winger away with a defence-splitting pass. After playing in just 10 League games for The Lions in the club's promotion season of 1962, many fans were surprised by his transfer to Second Division Bristol Rovers in December 1961. After his playing career was over, Dave tried his hand as a manager of both Brentwood and Chelmsford and latterly he was associated with the licensing trade.

Joey Broadfoot shows his team-mates how to lift weights.

Millwall players showing off their chests for the front cover of *Soccer Star*, in a training break at The Den. Flexing their muscles on this occasion are, from left to right, back row: Ray White, Jeff Howells, Ray Brand, Reg Davies, Pat Brady, Dennis Jackson. Front row: Joe Broadfoot, Sammy Wilson, Alf Ackerman, Barry Pierce, Ron Heckman.

Cheshire-born David Jones joined Millwall just before the Christmas of 1959, having appeared in Crewe Alexandra's first team in the old Third Division North as a sixteen-year-old. Prior to the commencement of the 1956/57 season he was signed by Birmingham City and managed to appear in the First Division on 9 occasions. After two seasons at St Andrews he moved to the Millwall, and by the end of the campaign he had played in 9 League games for The Lions. Over the next four years Jones would become a regular in Millwall's first eleven, and form a lethal partnership with Peter Burridge – their pairing for the club saw them hit an incredible 104 goals from 173 League matches. When Burridge departed in the summer of 1962, Jones would complete another two seasons at The Den. He was, however, one of the casualties of The Lions' relegation in 1964, and it was sad to see him becoming the focus of the crowd's displeasure in his last season with the club. A Fourth Division championship winner in 1962, David Jones' overall record with Millwall was 75 goals in 179 games.

A shot taken from the Cold Blow Lane terracing, with the half-finished stand to the left.

Millwall FC, 1959/60. From left to right, back row: J. Strain, R. Brand, S. Morgan, R. Davies, B. Paul, A. Moyse, D. Harper, R. White. Third row: A. Ackerman, L. Vaessen, R. Humphries, B. Pierce, P. Brady, S. Wilson, A. Crowshaw. Second row: R. Brady, D. Bumpstead, H. Redmond, J. Hutton, J. Howells, D. Jackson, R. Heckman. Front row: B. Bell, J. Broadfoot. The Lions finished fifth in the Fourth Division, winning 18 matches, drawing 17 and losing 11; they scored 84 goals and conceded 61. The leading scorer was Alf Ackerman with 18 goals.

Reg Davies was of muscular build and not very tall for a goalkeeper. His agility in the last line of Millwall's defence, however, more than made up for his lack of height and earned him the sobriquet 'The Cat' from an appreciative Cold Blow Lane crowd. Reg, a native of the Black Country, had already played for two clubs in his own locality, West Bromwich Albion and Walsall, and it was from the latter that he joined The Lions in May 1958. In the course of the next five seasons, Reg would hold down his place in the first team with a great level of consistency, missing out only occasionally when he was injured or suspended. Reg's indiscipline came about more often than not when he disagreed over an opposing forward's attitude. Nonetheless, Reg, for all his faults, was an outstanding custodian for Millwall and a great favourite with the fans. After leaving The Den with 218 games under his belt, he saw further service with Leyton Orient (twice) and Port Vale.

Three
The Super 1960s

Millwall FC, 1960/61. From left to right, back row: R. Brady, D. Harper, R. Burrows, D. Jackson, B. Pierce, H. Redmond, T. Ritchie, J. Lovett, V. Rickis. Third row: J.R. Smith (manager), A. Ackerman, R. Brand, A. Anderson, W. Waters, R. Davies, D. Jones, L. Burns, D. Bumpstead, R. Gray (assistant manager), H. Butler (assistant trainer). Second row: J. Blackman (trainer), J. Seed (director), Dr D. Eppel, G.S. Kenure (director), F.C. Purser (chairman), N. Weedon (director), T. Caygill (director), G. Borland (secretary). Front row: W. Hinshelwood, J. Broadfoot, R. Taylor, P. Brady, A. Spears, L. Vaessen, J. Howells. Millwall finished this campaign in sixth position in the Fourth Division, winning 21 games, drawing 8 and losing 17; they scored 97 goals and conceded 86. The top scorer was Peter Burridge with 35 goals.

Millwall legend Jack Fort, now a groundsman, discusses the playing surface with Peter Burridge and Ron Gray. Jack's association with Millwall, as a player went back to before the First World War. Peter's record as a striker was amazing, with 44 goals from 93 games in all competitions. Ron Gray had two spells as manager of The Lions, from 1956 to 1958 and 1961 to 1963.

Alan Spears and Peter Burridge take a jog around the pitch. Alan was a former England schoolboy international, and joined Millwall from Newcastle in 1960 to fill the problematic outside-left role. After a decent first season, his appearances in the first team became less frequent over the next two years, and he departed for Lincoln City in 1963.

The Millwall team that lined up against the now defunct Accrington Stanley at Peel Park in 1960/61. From left to right, back row: D. Harper, G. Townend, R. Brand, R. Davies, D. Jones, D. Jackson. Front row: L. Vaessen, W. Hinshelwood, P. Burridge, H. Redmond, A. Ackerman. The score in this match was 3-3, with Jones getting the first two goals and Burridge scoring the third.

Des Anderson, a wing-half, signed from Hibernian at the beginning of the 1961/62 season. A former Scottish schoolboy international, he played in just two games during The Lions' promotion campaign, but following Bumpstead's transfer and Harper's injury problems, Des found himself a more regular first team member over the next two seasons.

Triumphant at Barrow as Millwall become Fourth Division champions. Hero of the hour, Peter Burridge, holds the trophy.

Tommy Wilson turned out to be one of Millwall's finest post-war captures when he was signed from Falkirk for £750. Originally brought in as cover for the dominant Ray Brady, Tom would make a place in the middle line of The Lions' first team his own. A cool and commanding figure, he was rarely flustered and always seemed to clear the lines without too much difficulty. Wilson was one of the 'Magnificent Seven' in the side that would equal and then surpass Reading's record for the longest run of unbeaten home League games – which Millwall reached with a run of 59 games in 1966. Unfortunately, just when The Lions were building up the squad to challenge for promotion, manager Benny Fenton sold Tom to Hull City for £18,000, and leading scorer Bobby Hunt to Ipswich Town in November 1967 – when a few days earlier Fenton had been quoted as saying that none of his players were for sale.

Millwall FC, 1962/63. From left to right, back row: F.C. Purser (chairman), B. Nelan (director), H. Bulter (assistant trainer), H. Cripps, T. Wilson, D. John, R. Davies, K. Beswick, D. Anderson, R. Brady, R. Gray (manager), J. Blackman (trainer). Middle row: J. Broadfoot, D. Harper, G. Townend, P. Terry, H. Obeney, P. Brady, D. Jones, A. Spears, J. Gilchrist. Bottom row: R. Kerr, R. Ward, J. Stocks, T. McQuade. Millwall finished sixteenth in the Third Division, winning 15, drawing 13 and losing 18 games; they scored 82 goals and conceded 87. Pat Terry was top scorer with 18 – just beating J. Broadfoot and D. Jones, who both had 17.

Pat Terry in action against Peterborough, in April 1963, which saw the Posh take the points, courtesy of a 1-0 win. Pat was one of the finest headers of a football; although not very tall for his position, his immaculate timing in leaping for the ball brought him many fine headed goals.

Millwall FC, 1963/64. From left to right, back row: D. Harper, D. John, H. Cripps, J. Stocks, A. Stepney, T. Wilson, J. Gilchrist, M. Foster, H. Obeney. Front row: F.C. Purser (chairman), D. Jones, P. Terry, G. Townend, R. Gray (manager), J. Haverty, J. McLaughlin, N.G. Weedon (director). Millwall finished twenty-first and were relegated to the Fourth Division. They had lost 22 games, won 14 and drawn 10; conceding 67 goals and scoring 53. The top scorer was Pat Terry with 10 goals.

The new manager and chairman Mickey Purser watch the team beat Crewe Alexandra 1-0, with a penalty goal from John McLaughlin. At the end of this season (1963/64) both Millwall and Crewe would be relegated.

An innovation by new manager Billy Gray was to introduce ballet exercises to the players' training routine – not the sort of thing one would expect to see in the Cold Blow Lane neighbourhood. Gray's reasoning went along the lines that as teams tried to emulate the Continental style of football, the players should acquire the suppleness of many foreign footballers. Millwall employed the services of Miss Doreen Hermitage, a well-known dancer at the time, to put the players through their paces with the relevant exercises, with a particular emphasis on balance, which would become part of their regular training schedule. Some of the players pictured here with Doreen are Joe Haverty, Harry Cripps and Gary Townend.

Billy Gray trying out the all-weather training ground at the back of The Den (at the Ilderton Road end).

Alex Stepney came to Millwall from Tooting & Mitcham and was thought to be Millwall's best ever 'keeper. An ever-present in the League for nearly three seasons, he made 158 appearances, only missing the last game of 1965/66. He achieved 3 England under-23 caps in this time. Stepney moved to Chelsea for £50,000 in May 1966, but made only one appearance before moving to Manchester United in September. The rest, as they say, is history as he went on to win a full England cap as well as League Championship, FA Cup and European Cup winners' medals.

Millwall FC, 1964/65. From left to right, back row: W. Gray (manager), J. Gilchrist, R. Dwight, D. Harper, A. Stepney, T. Wilson, D. John, H. Curran, J. Blackman (trainer). Middle row: R. Senior, J. Whitehouse, B. Snowdon, D. Jones, W. Neil. Front row: A. Cheeswright, B. Rowan. The Lions finished second in the Fourth Division, winning 23 games, drawing 16 and losing 7; they scored 78 goals and conceded 45. The top scorer was Hugh Curran with 18.

Millwall's celebrate their 2-0 FA Cup victory over First Division Fulham in front of 31,000. From left to right, at the back: D. Harper, B. Rowan, D. John, T. Wilson, H. Curran, R. Gough. Below: A. Stepney, H. Cripps, J. Gilchrist, D. Jones.

Jubilant scenes from The Lions' dressing room after clinching the runners-up spot in the last Fourth Division match of the 1964/65 season, in which Millwall defeated Notts County at Meadow Lane 2-1. Forty-eight hours previously, they had defeated Wrexham 1-0 in Wales to set up a thrilling climax to the season's end. The Millwall supporters who swelled the attendance at Nottingham that night were to witness to the club's meteoric rise up the divisions over the following two years. Celebrating with their cups of tea are, at the top of the picture, Jim Ryan (8 appearances/1 goal) and Barry Rowan (35/8). Next down are Tommy Wilson (40/2), Kenny Jones (24/3), Brian Snowdon (19/-), Mickey Brown (12/1), Alex Stepney (46/-), John Gilchrist (29/1), and Ray Gough (13/-). In front are chairman Mickey Purser, Hugh Curran (39/18), Lennie Julians (34/15), Dennis John (37/6), Chris Clarke (14/3), and John Rickard (director), and, right at the the front in his playing kit, is manager Billy Gray (8/-), the man who would lead Millwall to this promotion and one the following year, before resigning to take over at London rivals Brentford. The Lions League record that season was P46 W23 D16 L7 F78 A45 Pts 62 – just one point behind champions Brighton & Hove Albion.

July 1965, and welcoming the new coach, Bill Dodgin Jnr, for pre-season training at The Den are the club's doctor, director Bill Nelan, and chairman Mickey Purser. Bill Nelan was a very affable man and always had time to speak to the supporters. A River Thames dumb barge operator, he would name his craft after the Millwall players, and some of those Lions honoured were Jimmy Jinks, Charlie Hurley, Harry Cripps and Alex Stepney. These barges would operate mainly in the timber trade of the Surrey Commercial Dock, a location where Millwall would draw a vast amount of their support. Mickey Purser was a local businessman who ran car showrooms and a driving school based along the Old Kent Road – a venue much vandalised by so-called supporters, frustrated by the club's lack of ambition or the team's dismal performances, who would take it upon themselves to vent their anger upon Purser's premises.

Billy Gray gets down to work in his office as he plans Millwall's promotion from Division Three in the 1965/66 season.

Cheers! Millwall players celebrate with cups of tea at Meadow Lane after beating Notts County to become Fourth Division runners-up. Barry Rowan scored the winner in the 2-1 victory. From left to right: W. Gray (player-manager), L. Julians, D. John, H. Cripps, K. Jones, H. Curran, B. Rowan, T. Wilson, B. Snowdon, C. Clarke, J. Gilchrist, A. Stepney, R. Gough.

Millwall FC, 1965/66. From left to right, back row: L. Julians, H. Cripps, K. Jones, A. Stepney, J. Gilchrist, T. Wilson. Front row: G. Jacks, B. Rowan, B. Snowdon, C. Clarke, M. Brown. For the second season running, Millwall finished as runners-up and were again promoted, this time into the Second Division. They had won 27 games, drew 11 and lost 8; scoring 76 goals and conceding 43. The leading scorer was Len Julians with 22. This photo was taken before the start of the second round FA Cup tie at Hereford in December 1965, a game which Millwall lost 0-1.

Millwall chairman Mickey Purser admires the scaffolding that will hold the huge forty foot TV screens for the first live broadcast of a football match, which took place on Friday 28 January 1966 and featured the whole of the Third Division match between Workington and Millwall. This meant that, in a way, the new £8,000 signing from York City, Eamonn Dunphy (centre), would make his 'home' debut, although playing 300 miles away.

The Millwall players promoted to the Second Division at the first attempt celebrating in the dressing room. From left to right, standing: J. Blackman (trainer), T. Wilson, B. Snowdon, K. Jones, A. Stepney, H. Cripps. J. Gilchrist, D. John, W. Gray (manager). Kneeling: M. Brown, B. Rowan, E. Dunphy, G. Jacks, W. Neil, L. Julians.

Millwall's captain, Bryan Snowdon, leads out the 1965/66 promotion-winning team to the applause of the Mansfield players. This was the last home game of the season and also the final appearance as a Lion for goalkeeper Alex Stepney.

Joe Broadfoot emerged from Millwall's recently formed youth team and signed as a professional in February 1958. He made his League debut at eighteen and established himself as a first team regular. A fast and skilful winger with quality crosses, he was sold to Ipswich Town for £16,000 in October 1963. Joe returned to The Den in the close season of 1966, but was back at Portman Road by the time Millwall visited Ipswich the following April.

Millwall's return to the Second Division in 1966 came eighteen years after the club had last competed at that level, and during the first half of the 1966/67 season they were on course to beat Reading's unbeaten home League run. One of the games included in this epic sequence was against Cardiff City on 29 October. This game marked the home debut of Dougie Baker, the Lewisham-born striker who had been signed from Arsenal the previous summer. Doug is seen here being denied by Cardiff goalkeeper Wilson, but the youngster had the last laugh later when he scored the only goal of the game. Unfortunately, Baker would only play five games for The Lions before leaving The Den during the following close season.

The ninety minutes played on a Saturday afternoon are the culmination of the hard work put in at the training ground, as Bryan Snowdon, Ken Jones (left) and Harry Cripps (right) can verify in this photograph.

The Millwall team training at Deptford Park before the big cup-tie against Tottenham Hotspur in the 1966/67 season. From left to right, standing: W. Neil, H. Cripps, J. Gilchrist, K. Jones, L. Leslie, A. Willey. Squatting: M. Brown, R. Hunt, B. Snowdon, E. Dunphy, D. Baker, L. Julians. They went on to finish the season eighth in the Second Division, winning 18 games, drawing 9 and losing 15; they scored 49 goals and conceded 58. The leading scorer, for the second year running, was Len Julians with 17.

The 'Magnificent Seven' – from left to right (players only): Harry Cripps, Tommy Wilson, John Gilchrist, Ken Jones, Bryan Snowdon, Len Julians, Billy Neil. All of these players received a commemorative lighter from FA official Mr Shipman for the record 59 home games without defeat.

63

Millwall at Blackpool in 1967/68. From left to right, standing: K. Jones, D. Burnett, B. Kitchener, L. Leslie, D. Plume, H. Cripps, B. Hunt. Sitting; K. Weller, D. Possee, T. Wilson, E. Dunphy, B. Neil. Millwall finished the season in seventh place with 14 wins, 17 draws and 11 defeats; they scored 62 goals and conceded 50. The leading scorer was Keith Weller with 14 goals.

A toast to the Queen: Millwall players, directors and celebrities pictured after a friendly against The Internationals Club XI. From left to right: Bill Nelan (director), Mickey Purser (chairman), Des O'Connor, Guest, Guest, Jimmy Tarbuck, Benny Fenton (manager), John Gilchrist.

Chairman Micky Purser chats to Brian Conlon(left) at a photo-shoot in July 1968. Conlon was signed from Darlington in November 1967 after he scored one of the goals that knocked Millwall out of the League Cup. He made his debut against Crystal Palace and scored, along with Georgie Jacks (right), in the 2-2 draw in front of 30,000 at Selhurst Park.

Millwall FC, 1968/69. From left to right, standing: J. Gilchrist, H. Cripps, K. Jones, B. King, B. Kitchener, D. Burnett, B. Nichol. Sitting: R. Plume, D. Possee, K. Weller, B. Conlon, G. Jacks, W. Neil, E. Dunphy. This side finished the season in tenth position in the Second Division, winning 17, drawing 9 and losing 16 games; they scored 57 goals and conceded 49. The leading scorer was again Keith Weller with 16 goals – beating his strike partner Derek Possee by one.

Millwall Reserves, 1968/69. From left to right, back row: J. Blackman (trainer), A. Garner, B. Brown, A. Dorney, B. King, K. Walden, D. Plume, J. Barrett (coach). Seated: D. Armstrong, F. Peterson, J. Smith, G. Duck, D. O'Leary. This side won the London Mid-week League for a record third time:

P	W	D	L	F	A	PTS	POS	
1966/67 32	24	5	3	102	37	53	First
1967/68 28	14	7	7	67	49	35	First
1968/69 12	11	0	1	37	10	22	First

Aladdin promotes the Lewisham Town Hall Christmas pantomime with the players before their cup-tie with Leicester … who are no doubt hoping that some of the magic will rub off on them.

Benny Fenton introduces Andy Nelson (*far left*) to players Billy Neil, Keith Weller, and Ken Jones at the pre-season photo call.

The team before the opening game of the 1969/70 season at Bolton on 9 August. From left to right, standing: B. Brown, B. Kitchener, B. King, H. Cripps, D. Burnett, B. Dear. Kneeling: W. Neil, G. Bolland, K. Weller, G. Jacks, E. Dunphy, F. Peterson.

Millwall FC, 1969/70. From left to right, back row: B. Mullen, A. Garner, R. Howell, D. O'Leary, B. Salvage, B. Nicholls, B. Neil. Third row: A. Nelson(trainer/coach), G. Bolland, K. Jones, B. Kitchener, B. King, H. Cripps, B. Brown, D. Burnett, J. Blackman (trainer/physiotherapist). Second row: D. Possee, J. Gilchrist, K. Weller, W. Nelan (director), F.C. Purser (chairman), B.R.V. Fenton (manager), D.G. Borland (secretary), G. Jacks, E. Dunphy, A. Dorney. Front row: M. Hobbs, S. Brown, D. Allder, J. Godfrey, A. Ballard, P. Lally, G. Duck, J. Flaherty, T. Sampson. Millwall finished tenth, winning 15 games, drawing 14 and losing 13; they scored 56 goals and conceded the same number. The leading scorer was Derek Possee with 18.

Barry Bridges in action on his debut in a 0-0 draw against Sunderland. The photograph shows the north terrace which, before the roof was added in the early 1920s, was known as The Kop. Barry had been the subject of transfer speculation long before he joined Millwall in September 1970. A much-travelled striker who saw service with Chelsea, Birmingham City and Queen's Park Rangers, Bridges was also a former England international.

Four

The Suffering 1970s

The Millwall team at Brisbane Road in 1970/71, for a game against Leyton Orient. The match finished as a 0-0 draw. From left to right, standing: S. Brown, B. King, B. Kitchener, B. Brown, H. Cripps, D. Burnett, A. Dorney. Kneeling: G. Bolland, D. Possee, D. Allder, B. Bridges, E. Dunphy. This side finished eighth in the Second Division, winning 19, drawing 9 and losing 14; they scored 59 goals and conceded 42. The leading scorer was Barry Bridges with 15.

Millwall FC, 1971/72. From left to right, back row: B. Brown, D. Burnett, D. Mackie, B. King, A. Dorney, G. Bolland. Middle row: W. Holmes, S. Brown, D. Coxhill, G. Jacks, W. Neil. Front row: B. Bridges, D. Possee, H. Cripps, E. Dunphy, D. Allder. Millwall finished third in the Second Division, only one point from promotion to the top flight of English football. The Lions won 19 matches, drew 17 and lost 6; scoring 64 goals and conceding 46. Derek Possee was the top scorer with 15.

The players in preparation for The London Footballers' Athletics Championship at Crystal Palace Recreation Centre, with Bryan King, Doug Aller, Gordon Bolland and Barry Bridges showing their prowess at hurdling.

Millwall celebrate their 2-0 win over Everton in the FA Cup during the 1972/73 season. From left to right, standing: J. Blackman, H. Cripps, F. Saul, D. Burnett, B. Kitchener, G. Bolland, L. Leslie (coach), B. Fenton (manager), A. Wood, E. Dunphy. Seated: A. Dorney, B. King, B. Brown, D. Allder, S. Brown.

The players wait patiently for the FA Cup draw after their defeat of Everton; Millwall drew Wolves away in the next round. The players are, from left to right, back row: T. Sampson, W. Neil, M. Kelly, W. Holmes, D. Allder, B. King, B. Kitchener, B. Brown. Front row: A. Dorney, S. Brown, A. Wood, E. Dunphy, H. Cripps.

Millwall FC, 1972/73. From left to right, back row: D. Burnett, H. Cripps, G. Bolland, B. King, B. Kitchener, D. Smethurst, A. Dorney. Middle row: W. Holmes, D. Allder, B. Bridges, B. Brown, S. Brown, T. Sampson, D. Coxhill, E. Dunphy. Front row: D. Possee, W. Neil, F. Saul, A. Wood. Millwall finished eleventh in the table, winning 16, drawing 10 and losing 16 of their games. The leading scorer was Gordon Bolland with 19 goals.

Millwall's lack of a physical striker was probably one of the reasons The Lions narrowly failed to gain promotion to Division One in 1972. To rectify this problem, manager Benny Fenton went out that summer to buy Alf Wood from Shrewsbury Town for £45,000. Wood, whom many would describe as the archetypal Millwall centre forward, appeared 115 times for The Lions and scored 45 goals.

Goalkeeper turned wicketkeeper Bryan King tries to catch out batsman Derek Possee.

A more informal shot of the team in 1972/73. From left to right, back row: B. King, D. Allder, B. Kitchener, G. Bolland, F. Saul, H. Cripps, A. Dorney, A. Wood, L. Leslie (coach). Front row: E. Dunphy, D. Burnett, S. Brown, B. Brown. The mascot is Mathew Harrison, with Leo.

Millwall FC, 1973/74. From left to right, back row: A. Wood, S. Webb, R. Wainwright, D. Smethurst, F. Saul, T. Sampson, R. Pittaway, B. Kitchener, B. King, M. Kelly, E. Jones. Front row: G. Hill, K. Enver, E. Dunphy, A. Dorney, D. Donaldson, H. Cripps, D. Burnett, S. Brown, B. Brown, G. Bolland, D. Allder. Millwall finished twelfth in the Second Division, winning 14, drawing 14, and losing 14 games; they scored and conceded 51 goals. The leading scorer was Alf Wood with 21.

Gordon Hill, who was known as 'Merlin', had outstanding skills that earned him international recognition. The Millwall youngster entertained the fans with some incredible shooting and dribbling and it was not long before scouts from the big clubs noticed him. He duly signed for Manchester United in November 1975 for £70,000. During his career, Hill played at every stage for England – as an amateur, youth, under-23, England B and full international (with 6 caps). He made 92 (8) appearances for Millwall and scored 22 goals.

The players get in a charity mood before the FA Cup game against Scunthorpe.

Millwall FC, 1974/75. From left to right, standing: W. Neil, M. Kelly, D. Donaldson, D. Smethurst, B. King, A. Dorney, A. Cox, B. Clarke, W. Kellock, G. Bolland, B. Kitchener, A. Wood, B. Fenton (manager), L. Leslie (coach). Seated: D. Allder, B. Brown, F. Saul, H. Cripps, K. Enver, E. Jones, S. Brown, T. Sampson, G. Hill. Millwall finished twentieth in the table and were relegated to the Third Division, having won 10, drawn 12 and lost 20 of their games; they conceded 56 goals and scored 44. The top scorer was Brian Clarke with only 7 goals.

New signings Tommy Baldwin (from Chelsea), Ray Goddard (Orient) and Mike Dillon (Spurs). Baldwin and Dillon both came in on loan, whereas Goddard would go on to become a more than adequate replacement for Bryan King while at Cold Blow Lane.

Brian Clarke and Chris Kelly are right on the ball in the latter's home debut v. Oldham on 8 February 1975. The score was 0-0. Kelly had joined Millwall from Leatherhead when their FA Cup run ended. Kelly, known as the 'Leatherhead Lip', failed to live up to any sort of reputation at The Den, and was soon back with the Surrey club.

Millwall FC, 1975/76. From left to right, standing: W. Neil, M. Wright, E. Jones, R. Evans, B. King, R. Goddard, J. Moore, A. Dorney, D. Donaldson, A. Hart. Seated: G. Jago (manager), F. Saul, P. Summerill, A. Hazell, A. Welsh, B. Kitchener, T. Brisley, B. Fairbrother, G. Borg, T. Foley (assistant manager). Millwall finished third in the Third Division and were promoted back to the Second Division at the first attempt. They won 20 matches, drew 16 and lost 10 goals; goals for 54, against 43. Joint top scorers, with 8 goals each, were Phil Summerill and Gordon 'Merlin' Hill, with Hill only playing 15 games before being sold to Manchester United.

Chris McGrath, a loan signing from Tottenham Hotspurs, scored on his Millwall debut at Gillingham in February 1976. This game was the only one in which Chris was on the losing side. Whilst at The Den he managed to add to his tally of International caps when he appeared for Northern Ireland against Israel in March that year.

The Millwall team parade in front of the fans before the last home game of the 1975/76 season against Peterborough. The Lions won 2-0, with goals from Phil Walker and Chris McGrath, to put them in third place, although they had to wait till the last game of the season at Swindon to be sure of beating Brighton to third spot. They duly beat the Wiltshire side 2-0 and were promoted to the Second Division.

Tony Kinsella signs his contract, watched by his proud father and club secretary Gordon Borland (right). Tony was a member of the youth side who won the FA Youth Cup in 1979. He made a total of 102 appearances for Millwall and scored 2 goals.

Millwall FC, 1976/77. From left to right, back row: W. Neil (assistant coach), A. Welsh, L. Templeman, S. Hamberger, D. Donaldson, R. Goddard, N. Johns, J. Moore, P. Summerill, T. Lee, A. Dorney, J. Blackman (physiotherapist). Middle row: G. Jago (manager), B. Salvage, T. Shanahan, T. Brisley, J. Seasman, B. Kitchener, A. Hazell, P. Walker, R. Evans, G. Borg, B. Fairbrother, T. Foley (assistant manager). Front row: R. Austin, G. Morris, T. Maurice, S. Savage. Millwall finished tenth with 15 wins, 13 draws and 14 defeats; they scored 57 goals and conceded 53. The leading scorer was John Seasman with 14.

This classic Millwall v. Wolves encounter on New Year's Day 1977, was an end-to-end, thrilling spectacle. It was witnessed by almost 17,000 fans who suffered under some torrential rain during the course of the match. Seen here are Hibbert and Pierce of Wolves attempting to clear a Millwall attack, watched by Lions strikers John Seasman and Barry Fairbrother. The game ended in a 1-1 draw.

Millwall FC, 1977/78. From left to right, back row: T. Brisley, J. Moore, C. Harris, P. Walker. Middle row: G. Jago (manager), T. Lee, A. Tagg, R. Goddard, N. Johns, D. Donaldson, J. Alexander, T. Foley (assistant manager). Front row: J. Seasman, A. Hazell, B. Kitchener, B. Hamilton, B. Chambers, P. Summerill. Millwall finished sixteenth, winning 12, drawing 14 and losing 16 of their games; they conceded 57 and scored 49 goals. The leading scorer was Ian Pearson with 9.

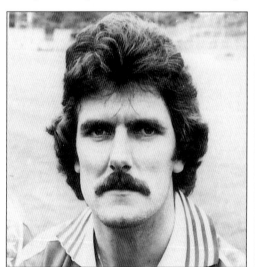

Left: Brian Chambers transferred to Millwall from Luton Town. Born in Newcastle, he made the League grade with Sunderland and had a spell with Arsenal but he only played once. He made 63 (5 substitute) appearances and scored 10 goals for The Lions. *Right*: Terry Brisley was a midfielder who played 142 League games for Orient before joining Millwall in part exchange for Doug Allder in June 1975, a move that realised a boyhood dream of playing for the side he supported and still follows to this day.

At the start of manager George Petchey's first full season at Cold Blow Lane, 1978/79, he and the supporters were hoping that his charges would storm up the Second Division table, and avoid the flirtation with relegation that had marked the previous campaign – disaster had only been averted when Millwall won the last six matches. Given some money to spend by a grateful board of directors, Petchey brought in John Mitchell from Fulham for around £100,000. He had been the hero of the Cottagers' run to the 1975 FA Cup final, but was now looking for a new challenge. However, in three injury-strewn years at The Den, John never really got going, and he left when the accumulated physical damage finally caught up with him. He later became manager of his home town club, St Albans City. John Hamilton (*middle*) was a rarity at The Den, being a Scot and the first for some time to be signed directly from a Scottish club. Hamilton picked up a few honours while with Rangers, but was given a free transfer. Petchey immediately stepped in to sign the midfielder, but the move did not work, as he failed to settle. After just three appearances he was hankering for a move back north of the border, which came when St Johnstone acquired his services.

Left: John Alexander was a forward who played for Cheshire schoolboys before moving to London to get a degree at London University. Recommended by Eamon Dunphy, he made his debut against Charlton whilst still a non-contract player. Alexander gained his degree in July 1977 and signed as a full professional, making 12(5) appearances and scoring 2 goals. *Right*: Jon Moore was born in Cardiff but started his career with Bristol Rovers. Although he never played for Rovers' first team, he moved to Millwall for £20,000 in December 1974 and played 135 games, scoring 1 goal.

Millwall *v.* Fulham; John Alexander gets between Fulham's Les Strong and the former England World Cup-winning captain Bobby Moore, with John Seasman close by.

The 1977/78 winners of the London Five-a-side Cup, who beat Queens Park Rangers 3-2 in the final, having already put out Orient and then Brentford 3-0 in the semi-final. Tony Hazell picked up the Player of the Tournament award. From left to right, back row: J. Seasman, A. Hazell, C. Dibble. Front row: N. Johns, D. Donaldson, P. Walker.

In 1978/79, Millwall won the capital's five-a-side tournament for the second year running, beating Crystal Palace in the final. Ironically, Tony Hazell – the Millwall captain the previous year – was in the Eagles team that were beaten 3-2. The Lions also defeated Chelsea 1-0 in the semi-finals and Orient 1-0 in the second round. From left to right: Phil Walker, Brian Chambers, D. Donaldson, Nicky Chatterton, Joycelyn Stevens (director of Express Newspapers), Pat Cuff, David Gregory.

At the end of the 1978/79 season there were contrasting scenarios at the club: the first team had been relegated while the Youth squad won the FA Youth Cup for the first time. Seen celebrating here with the cup and their tankards are, from left to right, back row: McKenna, Robinson, Massey (hidden), Roberts, O'Callaghan, Kinsella (hidden), Mehmet, Martin. Front row: Gale, Dibble, Coleman. Millwall's route to the final involved beating Slough 3-0 in the second round, Norwich 2-0 in the third round and Sunderland 2-1 in the fourth round. Nottingham Forest were The Lions' quarter-final opponents and they drew the first game 3-3, with the Millwall youngsters winning the replay 1-0. They then met Everton in the semi-final and drew the first leg 0-0, winning the second 2-0. In the final, against Manchester City, the first leg ended goal-less; The Lions were victorious in the second, 2-0.

Millwall FC, 1979/80. From left to right, back row: D. Donaldson, P. Roberts, P. Robinson, C. Dibble, N. Chatterton, D. Gregory. Middle row: A. Mckenna, D. Mehmet, P. Gleasure, P. Coleman, P. Cuff, A. Tagg, A. Kinsella. Front row: R. Adams (physiotherapist), M. Blythe, J. Lyons, A. Towner, G. Petchey (manager), J. Mitchell, K. O'Callaghan, J. Seasman, T. Long (assistant manager). Millwall finished fourteenth in the Third Division, winning 16 games, drawing 13 and losing 17; they scored 65 goals and conceded 59. The top scorer was John Lyons with 18.

The 1979/80 Millwall FC youth team. From left to right, back row: D. Horrix, D. Martin, P. Robinson. Middle row: R. Cross (coach), A. Wallace, C. Hemsley, P. Sansome, M. Hawkswell, D. Rose. Front row: A. Massey, A. Mckenna, P. Roberts, K. O'Callaghan, A. Kinsella.

Five

The Ups and Downs of the 1980s

Millwall FC, 1980/81. From left to right, back row: J. Bartley, J. Sweetzer, P. Coleman, D. Martin, P. Robinson, J. Sitton. Middle row: A. Massey, J. Mitchell, A. Tagg, J. Jackson, P. Gleasure, B. Kitchener, M. Blythe, A. McKenna. Front row: D. Gregory, D. Mehmet, P. Roberts, N. Chatterton, A. Kinsella, C. Dibble. Millwall finished this campaign in sixteenth position, winning 14, drawing 14 and losing 18 games; they conceded 60 goals and scored 43. Nicky Chatterton was top-scorer with 8 goals.

Millwall FC, 1981/82. From left to right, back row: D. Martin, D. Horrix, A. McKenna, J. Sitton, A. Massey, J. Bartley, J. Mitchell. Middle row: T. Long (trainer), C. Guthrie, P. Gleasure, B. Kitchener, P. Sansome, A. Tagg, R. Cross (coach). Front row: C. Dibble, P. Roberts, N. Chatterton, P. Anderson (player manager), A. West, P. Warman, A. Hayes. Millwall finished ninth in the Third Division, winning 18, drawing 13 and losing 15 games; they scored and conceded 62 goals. Top scorer was Dean Horrix with 15 goals.

Teddy Sheringham came through the youth ranks and signed professional forms in January 1984. Teddy holds the all-time scoring record for the club with 111 goals in 244 appearances (plus 18 as substitute). He won an England B cap and 11 youth caps whilst with Millwall. He was transferred to Nottingham Forest in 1991 and in August 1992 moved onto Tottenham Hotspurs for £2.1 million. Full international honours followed. In 1997 he signed for Manchester United, and won all the silverware imaginable to a young footballer. His greatest accolade was to be voted Player of the Year in 2001. He also made a surprising move back to White Hart Lane in the summer of 2001.

Millwall FC, 1982/83 youth team line-up. From left to right: B. Kitchener (manager), J. Neal, R. Green, N. Bewick, N. Coleman, C. Cowley, T. Ashby, E. Sheringham, P. Golding, D. Plumb, R. Wynter, N. Milo (coach), R. Pearson (chief scout).

The programme cover for a Football League Trophy final at Lincoln City. This was the only season in which the competition was played, and it provided Millwall with their first national trophy win. Contrary to the belief of many fans, any Football League club could enter the tournament and some sides from the top two divisions did participate – although not those in Europe or who thought that they would go through to the latter stages of the Football League Cup. Goals from Dean Neal (2) and Alan McLeary gave The Lions a 3-2 victory in this fixture.

Alan McLeary, Nick Chatterton (squatting) and Dean White with the Football League Trophy and the London Five-a-side Cup. Alan was a product of the club's youth system, while Nick was brought to the club in 1978 by former manager George Petchey. White was a former Chelsea youngster and was installed by George Graham to galvanize Millwall's midfield in 1982.

Millwall FC, winners of the London Five-a-side Cup, 1982/83. From left to right, back row: Andy Massey, Bobby Robson (guest), Paul Sansome, Joycelyn Stevens (director of the tournament's sponsor), Alan McLeary. Front row: Dean Neal, Roger Wynter, Teddy Sheringham. Millwall won the final, played against Brentford, 3-2. They also beat Charlton (3-2), West Ham (2-0), and Arsenal (3-1) in the semi-finals. Roger Wynter picked up the Player of the Tournament award, having scored 8 goals.

Millwall FC, 1982/83. From left to right, back row: A. McLeary, D. Horrix, A. West, P. Robinson, A. Massey. Middle row: T. Long (assistant manager), C. Speight (physiotherapist), D. Martin, T. Aylott, P. Gleasure, P. Sansome, K. Stevens, L. Madden, B. Kitchener (youth team coach), R. Cross (coach). Front row: A. Hayes, P. Roberts, S. Allardyce, P. Anderson (manager), N. Chatterton, W. Carr, P. Warman. Millwall finished in seventeenth position in the Third Division, having won 14 games, drawn 13 and lost 19; they scored 63 goals and conceded 77. The leading scorer was Dean Neal with 18.

Millwall FC, 1983/84. From left to right, back row: T. Foley (assistant manager), A. McLeary, P. Robinson, D. White, P. Wells, D. Cusack, P. Sansome, M. Nutton, D. Martin, G. Graham (manager). Front row: D. Stride, S. Lovell, K. Bremner, N. Chatterton, A. Otulakowski, D. Neal, A. Massey. Millwall finished the season in ninth position, winning 18 matches, drawing 13 and losing 15; goals scored 71, conceded 65. Kevin Bremner was top scorer with 15.

The Millwall youth team, 1983/84. From left to right, back row: E. Sheringham, N. Coleman, T. Fuller, B. Horne, D. Plumb, D. Lee, N. Ruddock. Kneeling: P. Gordon, D. James, J. Neal, P. Golding, L. Robinson.

The Neal brothers, Dean and John. John, the youngest of the two, was a Irish youth international who made 12 appearances for The Lions, scoring 1 goal. Dean, who made 152 appearances, scoring 62 goals, was recruited from Tulsa Roughnecks and looked set to establish himself as a Millwall hero. Unfortunately, he fell out with George Graham and was transferred to Southend United.

Kevin Bremner giving the opposing team's (in this case Wigan) defence a hard time as usual. Bremner was another of the bustling type of striker used by Millwall over the years. Despite a lack of finesse in his approach to the game, Kevin never gave less than 100 per cent during a match.

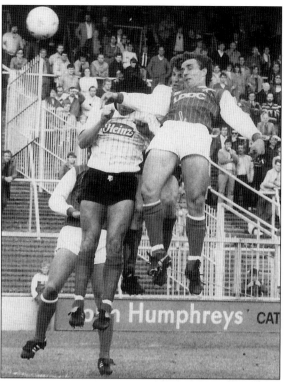

The Lions do their bit for public health in this promotional shot from the 1984/85 season. From left to right, top row: P. Sansome, J. Fashanu, L. Smith, P. Hinshelwood, J. Neal, M. Nutton. Bottom row: L. Briley, N. Chatterton, A. Kinsella, N. Coleman, D. Neal, S. Lovell.

Millwall celebrate after the 2-0 victory over Plymouth Argyle that sealed promotion to the Second Division at the end of 1984/85. From left to right, back row: A. Otulakowski, A. McLeary, J. Miller (physiotherapist), K. Stevens, L. Smith, D. Neal, G. Graham, D. Cusack, N. Chatterton, P. Sansome, S. Lovell, P. Hinshelwood, T. Kinsella, T. Foley. Front row: J. Fashanu, S. Lowndes, L. Briley.

Les Briley leads out the promotion-winning team, followed by that lion-hearted defender Dave Cusack and, in the 'whistle', the injured Steve Lovell, who finished up with 21 League goals – not bad for a converted full-back!

Millwall FC, 1984/85. From left to right, back row: T. Foley (assistant manager), L. Smith, K. Stevens, P. Robinson, M. Nutton, P. Sansome, D. Cusack, P. Wells, S. Lovell, D. Neal, A. McLeary, E. Sheringham, B. Carnaby (physiotherapist). Front row: B. Roffey, N. Chatterton, S. Lowndes, K. Bremner, A. Otulakowski, G. Graham (manager), N. Coleman, J. Neal, A. Kinsella, L. Briley, C. Cowley. This side finished the season in second place and were promoted to the Second Division, having won 26 matches, drawn 12 and lost 8; they scored 73 goals and conceded 42. The top scorer was Steve Lovell with 21 goals.

Millwall players of the future line up in this 1985/86 youth team photograph taken by Tom Green. From left to right, back row: G. Stevens (assistant coach), M. Marks, L. Robinson, N. Ruddock, B. Horne, D. Thompson, T. Webb, B. Potter, R. Cross (coach). Front row: P. Joyce, T. Booker, D. Morgan, G. Middleton, S. Sparham, P. Malcolm. Seven of these players progressed to the first team.

Millwall FC, 1985/86. From left to right, back row: T. Foley (assistant manager), J. Miller (physiotherapist), P. Robinson, P. Hinshelwood, M. Nutton, D. Fry, L. Smith, P. Sansome, A. McLeary, R. Wilson, G. Graham (manager). Front row: A. Kinsella, S. Lovell, S. Lowndes, A. Otulakowski, L. Briley, N. Coleman, N. Chatterton, J. Fashanu, W. Roffey. Millwall finished ninth in the Second Division, having won 17 matches, drawn 8 and lost 17; they scored 64 goals and conceded 65. The leading scorer was again Steve Lovell, with 14 goals.

The players applaud the crowd after the last game of the 1985/86 season, with Welsh international Steve Lowndes (left) no doubt wishing he had kept his shirt on.

94

Millwall FC, 1986/87. From left to right, back row: D. Mehmet, A. McLeary, P. Hinshelwood, K. Stevens, A. Walker, M. Nutton, M. Marks, D. Salman. Middle row: R. Cross (coach),N. Chatterton, N. Coleman, P. Sansome, B. Horne, T. Sheringham, S. Lovell, J. Miller (physiotherapist). Front row: D. Morgan, R. Wilson, D. Byrne, J. Docherty (manager),J. Leslie, S. Lowndes, L. Briley. Millwall finished sixteenth in the Second Division. They won 14 games, drew 9 and lost 19; scoring 39 and conceding 45 goals. Teddy Sheringham scored the most goals, with 13.

Nick Coleman was a reliable left-back who was forced to retire with a serious knee injury suffered during a pre-season friendly. He started at the club as a thirteen year old and signed professional terms under George Graham. Nick played 107 games for The Lions. He and Sean Sparham shared a testimonial game against Crystal Palace in August 1991, after both of their careers were cut short by injury.

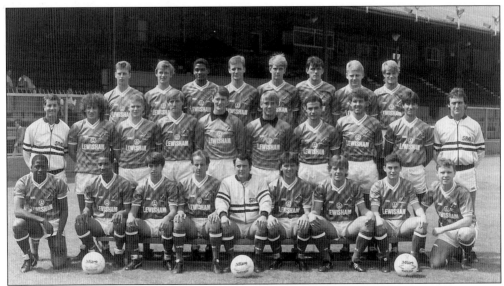

Millwall FC, 1987/88. From left to right, back row: K. Stevens, E. Sheringham, S. Anthrobus, A. Walker, D. Thompson, A. Cascarino, M. Marks, S. Wood. Middle row: F. McLintock (assistant manager), T. Hurlock, D. Mehmet, A. McLeary, P. Sansome, B. Horne, D. Salman, P. Coleman, J. Carter, R. Cross (coach). Front row: G. Lawrence, W. Reid, D. Morgan, L. Briley, J. Docherty (manager), D. Byrne, N. Coleman, S. Sparham, K. O'Callaghan. At the end of the season, this team had won the Second Division championship and Millwall was promoted to the top flight for the first time in their history. They won 25, drew 7 and lost 12 games, scoring 72 goals and conceding 52. The leading goal-scorer was again Teddy Sheringham, with 22 (beating Tony Cascarino by 2).

Best of mates – Teddy, Cally, Horny and Tel. All of these players gained international honours while at Millwall. Sheringham, Hurlock and Horne represented England at various levels, whilst the odd man out, O'Callaghan, appeared for the Republic of Ireland.

The Second Division champions celebrating their promotion at Boothferry Park, after beating Hull City 1-0 and securing the title. From left to right, standing: F. McLintock, S. Wood, J. Carter, (fan), K. Stevens, R. Cooke, G. Lawrence, D. Thompson, A. Cascarino, E. Sheringham, N. Coleman, D. Salman, K. O'Callaghan, T. Hurlock, D. Morgan. Crouching: B. Horne, D. Byrne.

The players step up to collect their medals and the Second Division trophy, prior to the last match of the 1987/88 season, against Blackburn Rovers. The Lancashire team won this fixture 4-1, to claim a play-off place at the expense of Millwall's South London neighbours, Crystal Palace.

Millwall FC, 1988/89. From left to right, back row: G. Lawrence, K. Stevens, E. Sheringham, S. Anthrobus, A. Cascarino, D. Thompson, N. Ruddock, D. Horrix, S. Wood. Middle row: P. Melville (physiotherapist), T. Hurlock, R. Cooke, A. McLeary, K. Branagan, B. Horne, D. Salman, K. O'Callaghan, J. Carter, R. Cross (coach). Front row: W. Reid, D. Morgan, A. Dowson, L. Briley, J. Docherty (manager), F. McLintock (assistant manager), D. Byrne, N. Coleman, S. Sparham, R. Chick. Millwall finished this campaign in tenth place in the First Division – the highest placing in their history – having won 14, drawn 11, and lost 13 games; they scored 47 goals and conceded 52. The top scorer was Tony Cascarino with 13 goals.

The programme cover for the game against Derby County, Millwall's first home game in the top flight. John Docherty and Les Briley are shown celebrating the previous season's championship triumph – although unfortunately the programme printers put the wrong year on the front cover!

Three heads are better than one – Tony Cascarino out-jumps Derby's Paul Blades.

An historic occasion as skippers Les Briley and Mark Wright lead out the teams for the first ever First Division match at The Den, in September 1988. The game went according to script, as Millwall won 1-0, with a goal from Teddy Sheringham.

Tony Cascarino scores his first of two goals against QPR to put Millwall top of the First Division.

Terry Hurlock in his England 'B' shirt – a fitting reward for a much-maligned player. He played against Switzerland, Iceland and Norway. The Iceland FA stated in their records that this was a full international match, but the English authorities at Lancaster Gate refused to upgrade the game to that level.

Millwall FC, 1989/90. From left to right, back row: D. Treacy, P. Babb, E. Sheringham, S. Torpey, D. Thompson, A. Cascarino, S. Anthrobus, M. Magill, S. Wood. Middle row: P. Melville (physiotherapist), G. Lawrence, P. Stephenson, A. McLeary, B. Horne, D. Horrix, K. Branagan, K. Stevens, T. Hurlock, W. Reid, F. Sibley (coach). Front row: D. Salman, J. Carter, S. Sparham, I. Dawes, J. Docherty (manger), L. Briley, F. McLintock (assistant manager), D. Morgan, K. O'Callaghan, A. Dowson, N. Coleman. Millwall ended this season with relegation, finishing twentieth in the First Division, having only won 5 matches, drawn 11 and lost 22; they conceded 65 goals and scored 39. The joint top scorers were Teddy Sheringham and Tony Cascarino with 9 apiece.

Dave Thompson gets in a tackle against Ian Rush in the match against Liverpool. It was Thompson who scored Millwall's only goal in this game, which The Lions lost 1-2 in November 1989.

Les Briley and Terry Hurlock take on Paul Gascoigne against Spurs. Ironically, in 1995 Gazza would tread the same path that Terry negotiated in the early 1990s, entering into the Glasgow Rangers midfield.

Les Briley, Millwall's 'Captain Fantastic' and a tenacious midfield battler, signed from Aldershot, where he had spent five seasons, in exchange for Andy Massey. Les has now played in all four divisions, also serving Hereford and Wimbledon. He made his debut against Orient in September 1984 and played a major role in Millwall's promotion to the top flight.

David Thompson scoring against Manchester City at The Den, 7 April 1990. His first-half header was not enough, however, as City equalised for a 1-1 draw, which came in a dreadful run of results for The Lions, who had recorded their last victory in the previous December. This sort of form had only one outcome, and Millwall were duly relegated at the season's end, after a slump of twenty games without a win.

Paul Goddard was The Lions' record signing from Derby in January 1990. Paul was signed to pep up the forward line, as he was leading scorer in the First Division at the time. Unfortunately, for a number of reasons, his stay at The Den was both unfulfilling for him and the club. His goals dried up, but not all of the blame should be heaped on Paul's shoulders. The style of Millwall's play did not really suit him; most service to him came in the air, when all he required was the ball on the ground.

Former chief scout, now caretaker-manager, Bob Pearson shakes hands with his new signing; Welsh international Malcolm Allen signed from Norwich for £400,000 on the transfer deadline in March 1990, along with Mick McCarthy (who came originally on loan).

Six

The 1990s and Recent Triumphs

Republic of Ireland tour team photograph, taken before the game with Cobh Ramblers. From left to right, back row: S. Torpey, J. McGlashan, B. Horne, D. Thompson, K. Cunningham, S. Wood. Front row: D. Treacy, L. Briley, M. Allen, D. Morgan, I. Dawes. Millwall played four matches and won all of them, the results being: Portadown (5-0), Cobh Ramblers (1-0), Shelbourne (5-1), Kilkenny (2-0).

Millwall FC, 1990/91. From left to right, back row: M. Allen, D. Treacy, P. Babb, E. Sheringham, S. Torpey, D. Thompson, M. McCarthy, K. Stevens, M. Magill, S. Wood, K. Cunningham. Middle row: S. Harrison (first team coach), P. Melville (physiotherapist), J. McGlashan, P. Stephenson, A. McLeary, B. Horne, P. Hucker, K. Branagan, P. Goddard, T. Hurlock, W. Reid, T. Walley (youth team coach), I. Evans (reserve team coach). Front row: D. Thompson, G. Waddock, J. Carter, S. Sparham, I. Dawes, B. Rioch (manager), I. McNeill (assistant manager), L. Briley, D. Morgan, K. O'Callaghan, A. Dowson, A. Rae, N. Coleman, A. Henry. Millwall finished fifth in the Second Division and reached the play-offs having won 20 games, drawn 13 and lost 13. The top scorer was Teddy Sheringham with an outstanding return of 33 goals. Unfortunately, Millwall were beaten by Brighton in the play-offs.

Millwall FC's Youth Cup championship-winning squad. From left to right, back row: B. Lee, L. Walker, A. Roberts, C. Emberson, J. Franklin, F. McArthur, D. Owen, M. Foran, D. Chapman, G. Rioch. Front row: T. Dolby, H. Dickson, P. Manning, C. Rogerson, S. Devine, B. Smith, R. Bedford. The team's path to the trophy was: (first round) Sutton 5-0 win, (second round) Swindon 1-0 win, (third round) Portsmouth 3-1 win, (fourth round) Plymouth 1-0 win, (fifth round) Wimbledon 1-1 and a 3-2 win in the replay, (semi-final first leg) West Ham 2-1 win, (second leg) 2-0 win, (final first leg) Sheffield Wednesday 3-0 win, (second leg) 0-0.

Millwall FC, 1991/92. From left to right, back row: A. McLeary, K. Stevens, C. Armstrong, J. McGlashan, D. Thompson, J. Humphrey, M. McCarthy. Middle row: S. Harrison (coach), J. McGinlay, J. Goodman, M. Falco, A. Davison, B. Horne, K. Cunningham, P. Stephenson, A. Rae, P. Melville (physiotherapist). Front row: J. Colquhoun, P. Kerr, I. Bogie, B. Rioch (manager), P. Barber, I. McNeil (assistant manager), C. Cooper, I. Dawes, M. Allen. Millwall finished the season in fifteenth position, winning 17, drawing 10 and losing 19 games; they scored 64 goals and conceded 71. The leading scorer was Alex Rae with 13.

Above: Cold Blow Lane in the 1960s, when the entrance fee was 5/-. This was a bleak brick-built street and opponents must have wondered what they let themselves in for, hence the record unbeaten run at home in the League. *Below:* Cold Blow Lane, just before it was demolished. A lick of blue and white paint, and the south stand entrances (where the old railway line used to be) made it a more welcoming place than it had been three decades before. Alas, it made way for new homes shortly after the last game at the ground on 8 May 1993. Millwall played a total of 1,827 first team games at the ground – of which they won 972 – and scored a total of 3,269 goals.

1992 Republic of Ireland tour team photograph, taken before the game with Cobh Ramblers at St Colman's Park. From left to right, back row: C. Cooper, P. Barber, K. Cunningham, C. Armstrong, J. Goodman, K. Stevens, K. Keller. Front row: I. Dawes, M. Allen, A. May, A. Roberts. Four matches were played on the tour: (28 July) Shelbourne 1-0 win, (30 July) Dundalk 1-1, (1 August) Cobh Ramblers 3-0 win, (4 August) Bohemians 2-0 win.

On 29 October 1992, the Millwall players were invited to an evening reception with the mayor of Lewisham, John O'Shea, to mark the final season at The Den. From left to right, back row: K. Keller, I. Dawes, J. Byrne (hidden), P. Barber, C. Cooper, P. Holsgrove, A. Davison, T. Dolby, M. Allen, A. Roberts, K. Johnstone (physiotherapist), J. Goodman, P. Melville (physiotherapist), K. Stevens, J. Moralee, A. May, A. Rae, R. Howard (scout). Front row: R. Burr (chairman), (mayoress), J. O'Shea (mayor), M. McCarthy (manager).

In 1992/93, an ex-Millwall XI turned out for Steve Gritt, whose daughter Hayley had undergone an operation to remove a brain tumour . The Lions played Charlton at The Valley and all proceeds went to the British Brain and Heart Foundation. From left to right, back row: B. Kitchener, B. Rowan, P. Gleasure, T. Wilson, H. Cripps, A. Massey, J. Moore, D. Allder, A. Dorney. Front row: Terry Gillam (a guest, who paid highest fee to play), D. Mehmet, T. Brisley, N. Chatterton, J. Seasman, P. Brady.

In 1992/93 the Millwall reserves became the Neville Ovenden Combination champions for the first time. They are pictured here at the old Den after the last reserve game, against Brighton. From left to right, back row: Holsgrove, McLeary, Dolby, Davison, A. McCarthy, Jeffrey, Saddington, McDonald (manager). Front row: Joseph, Redwood, Callaghan, Bogie, Gaynor, Kerr.

Millwall FC, 1992/93. From left to right, back row: P. Holsgrove, E. Verveer, K. Stevens, C. Armstrong, M. Foran, J. McGlashan, T. McCarthy, P. Stephenson, T. Dolby. Middle row: K. Johnstone (physiotherapist), P. Manning, J. McGinlay, J. Goodman, B. Horne, A. Davison, J. Donegan, K. Keller, C. Emberson, K. Cunningham, B. Lee, J. Humphrey, P. Melville (physiotherapist). Front row: A. May, A. Roberts, I. Bogie, A. Rae, M. McCarthy (manager), I. Evans (coach), P. Barber, C. Cooper, I. Dawes, M. Allen. Millwall finished seventh in Division One, having won 18, drawn 16 and lost 12 games; they scored 65 and conceded 53 goals. The leading scorer was Jamie Moralee with 15.

1992/93 was a remarkable season for the youth squad – they finished it as Southern Junior Floodlit champions, SEC League runners-up and Youth Cup semi-finalists (having beaten Manchester United 2-1 at Old Trafford). From left to right, back row: G. Stevens (physiotherapist), S. Walley, B. Thatcher, M. Kennedy, D. Wietecha, M. Middleton, D. Chapman, C. Luckett, A. Batsford (youth development officer), T. Walley (coach). Front row: V. Morgan, G. Pitcher, P Irvine, J. Wright, D. Francis, N. Gordon.

Alex Rae tussling against Derby. Alex ended his Millwall career with over 60 goals from his midfield position – only Nicky Chatterton and Joe Broadfoot (a winger) have also managed this feat.

Andy Roberts losing his kit in an end-of-season celebration. Andy was sold to rivals Crystal Palace in 1995 for over £2 million. Another product of the youth team, he would represent England at U-21 level on five occasions.

Jamie Moralee celebrating at Upton Park with his first-minute goal against West Ham.

Rhino scoring a rare goal – and probably the one he will savour the most – in the 2-2 draw with West Ham.

Kasey Keller receiving his Player of the Year award from his manager Mick McCarthy on 24 April 1993. Kasey became Millwall's first USA international; his appearance came a week after he made his football League debut, against Southend United in the last game of the 1991/92 season.

The first Millwall side to play at the New Den, against Sporting Lisbon on 4 August 1993, was, from left to right, back row: Kenny Cunningham, Andy Roberts, Carl Emberson, Kasey Keller, Tony McCarthy, Lee Luscombe, Keith Stevens (captain). Front row: Ian Bogie, John Kerr, Gavin Maguire, Ian Dawes, Malcolm Allen.

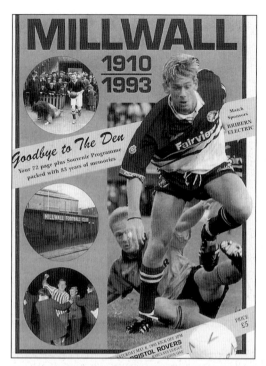

Programme cover for the game against Bristol Rovers on 8 May 1993 – the last at The Den. This was the club's most expensive programme, but a superb read and a fitting memento.

Millwall FC, 1993/94. From left to right, back row: P. Holsgrove, E. Verveer, J. Moralee, M. Foran, T. McCarthy, L. Luscombe, R. Huxford, T. Dolby. Middle row: K. Johnstone (physiotherapist), P. Manning, K. Stevens, J. Goodman, J. Saddington, K. Keller, C. Emberson, J. Byrne, J. Kerr, K. Cunningham, J. Humphry, P. Melville (physiotherapist). Front row: A. May, A. Roberts, I. Bogie, A. Rae, I. McDonald (reserve team coach), M. McCarthy (manager), I. Evans (coach), P. Barber, G. Maguire, I. Dawes, M. Allen. Millwall finished third in the Endsleigh League Division One and reached the play-offs for the second time (only to lose to Derby County). During the season they won 19, drew 17, and lost 10 games; scoring 58 goals and conceding 49. The top scorer was Alex Rae with 13.

The late Labour Party leader John Smith had the honour of opening the New Den on 4 August 1993. This photograph was taken before the opening match against Portuguese giants Sporting Lisbon, who were then managed by the former England coach Bobby Robson.

Millwall FC, 1994/95. From left to right, back row: J. Kerr, M. Kennedy, D. Mitchell, J. Goodman, G. Berry, T. McCarthy, K. Cunningham, C. Allen. Middle row: K. Johnstone (physiotherapist), K. Barry (kit man), K. Stevens, P. Van Den Hauwe, K. Keller, T. Carter, R. Huxford, D. Savage, I. McDonald (coach), P. Melville (physiotherapist). Front row: A. May, A. Roberts, M. Beard, A. Rae, I. Evans (coach), M. McCarthy (manager), P. Barber, J. Wright, I. Dawes, B. Thatcher. Millwall finished twelfth in Division One, winning 16, drawing 14 and losing 16 games; they scored 60 goals and conceded 60. The leading goalscorer this term was (again) Alex Rae with 10.

The first 1994/95 pre-season friendly, against Cambridge City on 23 July, saw the unveiling of the latest strip of red and black striped shirts. From left to right, back row: K. Stevens, P. Van Den Hauwe, A. May, G. Berry, K. Cunningham, D. Savage, J. Goodman. Front row: C. Allen, K. Keller, A. Rae, B. Thatcher.

John Kerr scores the first League goal at the New Den, against Southend United, on 22 August 1993. However, the joy of the occasion was short-lived, as the Shrimpers came back to secure victory with a four-goal salvo.

Keith Stevens tussles with his bitter rival, Stan Collymore of Nottingham Forest, in a televised League game in April 1994. Missing from the Forest team that day (through suspension) was Colin Cooper, whom The Lions had sold to the Reds the previous summer for £1 million.

Millwall's men at work; of these three Aussies – Alistair Edwards, Dave Mitchell and Jason Van Blerk – Ally was the odd one out in that he wasn't selected for his country whilst at The Den. He had previously been associated with Glasgow Rangers, as had Dave Mitchell. Jason, who spent nearly three seasons with Millwall, later saw service with Manchester City and West Bromwich Albion.

Millwall youth team squad, 1993/94. From left to right, back row: P. O'Neil, B. Thatcher, S. Aris, A. Cronin, N. Gordon, J. Wright, D. Francis. Front row: M. Kennedy, G. Pitcher, P. Irving, C. Luckett, S. Jones, M. Mulraney.

John Kerr carved himself a niche in Millwall's history, by not only scoring the first-ever goal at the New Den, but also the initial league goal, against Southend United. Another first for this American international was that he became the first Millwall substitute to score a hat-trick in a competitive match, against Derby County.

Millwall's comings and goings – Mark Kennedy, who was destined for Liverpool, with new arrival Kerry Dixon. Kerry was a very experienced striker, who was joining his sixth club when signing for The Lions. Mark had been a prolific goalscorer in youth team football at The Den, and he was yet another product of the club's youth policy.

Mark Beard and Mark Kennedy, the goalscoring heroes in a 2-0 win against Arsenal at Highbury. This victory was the first over the Gunners in the FA Cup since 1909.

Kasey Keller saves in the penalty shoot-out to put The Lions through to the FA Cup fifth round at Stamford Bridge.

Ben Thatcher tangles with Middlesbrough's Uwe Fuchs, who later joined Millwall. Like many signings during the Mark McCarthy management era, Fuchs never really lived upto the hype he had received while with Middlesbrough.

1995 Republic of Ireland tour team photograph, taken at Dalkey Park. From left to right, back row: M. Bennett, G. Berry, K. Stevens, B. Thatcher. Middle row: J. Van Blerk, A. Rogan, R. Newman, R. Bowry, D. Savage, S. Taylor. Bottom row: M. Doyle, D. Webber, D. Wietecha, K. Dixon, L. McRobert, R. Cadette. Millwall won all three matches that they played on the tour, beating Dundalk 3-1, Dalkey XI 3-0 and Shelbourne 2-0.

Millwall FC, 1995/96. From left to right, back row: M. Bennett, K. Dixon, A. Witter, U. Fuchs, J. Van Blerk, C. Malkin, G. Berry, A. Rogan, D. Webber. Middle row: K. Johnstone (physiotherapist), M. Harle, K. Stevens, R. Newman, D. Savage, J. Neilsen, K. Keller, D. Wietecha, A. Edwards, R. Bowry, M. Doyle, R. Cadette, I. McDonald (coach). Front row: P. O'Neil, B. Thatcher, S. Taylor, A. Rae, M. McCarthy (manager), I. Evans (first team coach), S. Forbes, L. McRobert, J. Connor, M. Beard. Millwall finished twenty-second in Division One and were relegated to Division Two, having won 13, drawn 13 and lost 20 games; they conceded 64 goals and scored 44. Leading scorer was Alex Rae with 13.

The Russians are coming – chairman Peter Meade and Mick McCarthy welcome Russian internationals Serguei Yuran (far left) and Vassili Kulkov from Spartak Moscow. They made their debut against Port Vale on 13 January 1996 in front of the biggest crowd of the season. Unfortunately The Lions went down 1-2 in this game and, to complete a disastrous time at the club, this pair of underachievers were one of the reasons Millwall were relegated that year.

1996 Scotland tour team photograph, taken at Ayr. From left to right, back row: K. Stevens, D. Sinclair, D. Savage, T. Carter, C. Malkin, R. Newman. Kneeling: S. Crawford, J. Dair, P. Hartley, mascot, J. Van Blerk, R. Bowry. The pre-season tour consisted of three matches: (27 July) Ayr Utd 3-4 defeat, (31 July) Stranraer 4-1 win, (3 August) Kilmarnock 2-4 defeat.

Millwall FC, 1996/97. From left to right, back row: T. Dolby, G. Berry, A. Rogan, J. Van Blerk, D. Webber, D. Savage, R. Sadlier, T. Witter, C. Malkin, S. Forbes, D. Canoville. Middle row: K. Johnstone (physiotherapist), S. Roche, L. McRobert, B. Markey, K. Stevens, J. Connor, K. Keller, A. Iga, D. Nurse, T. Carter, D. Keown, B. Bowry, L. Nightingale, M. Doyle, R. Cadette, K. Barry (kit man). Front row: I. McDonald (coach), M. Bircham, J. Dair, P. Hartley, G. Lavin, M. Harle, J. Nicholl (manager), M. Harvey (assistant manager), S. Aris, L. Neill, R. Newman, S. Crawford, D. Sinclair, R. Howard (chief scout). Millwall finished fourteenth in Division Two, winning 16, drawing 13 and losing 17 games; they scored 50 goals and conceded 55. The leading scorer was Steve Crawford with 11.

Millwall FC, 1997/98. From left to right, back row: S. Aris, D. Savage, A. McLeary, B. Law, A. Witter, D. Webber, K. Stevens, S. Fitzgerald, P. Sturgess, D. Hockton. Middle row: G. Chapman (reserve physiotherapist), K. Brown, R. Newman, G. Robertson, T. Carter, J. Connor, D. Nurse, D. Canoville, L. McRobert, R. Bowry, G. Docherty (physiotherapist). Front row: M. Bircham, L. Neill, J. Dair, P. Hartley, K. O'Callaghan, W. Bonds (manager), P. Holland (assistant manager), M. Doyle, B. Markey, G. Lavin, P. Allen. Millwall finished eighteenth in Division Two, winning 14, drawing 13, and losing 19 games, scoring 43 goals and conceding 54. The leading scorer for this campaign was Paul Shaw with 11.

Millwall's youngsters win the Kent Cup in 1997/98 with a 3-0 win against Sittingbourne – the goals coming from Dolan, Reid, and Ifill. This was the team's final year in the South East Counties League as the new Academy League started in the 1998/99 season. The jubilant team are, from left to right, standing: C. Clifford (physiotherapist), R. Bernard, B. Alimi, M. Phillips, P. Maguire, S. Reid, L. Williams, L. Odunsi, D. Gustave, P. Ifill, T. Powell, M. Flanagan (manager), J. Little, N. Milo (trainer). Kneeling: T. Cahill, R. Bull, P. Smith, J. Dolan, R. Davies, W. Mead. This photograph was taken by Karl Reynolds.

Millwall FC, 1998/99. From left to right, back row: A. Cook, D. Canoville, S. Fitzgerald, D. Hockton, S. Nethercott, B. Law, L. Cort, R. Sadlier, D. Savage, P. Ifill, P. Sturgess, R. Newman. Middle row: P. Maxwell (assistant physiotherapist), K. Brown, R. Ryan, M. Bircham, L. Neill, N. Spink, A. Gray, P. Smith, G. Robertson, K. Grant, S. Roche, R. Bowry, G. Docherty (physiotherapist). Front row; J. Carter, P. Shaw, J. McDougald, J. Stuart, A. McLeary (assistant manager), K. Stevens (manager), S. Gritt (reserve team coach), G. Lavin, N. Harris, T. Cahill, S. Reid. Millwall finished tenth in Division Two, winning 17, drawing 11 and losing 18 games; they scored 52 goals and conceded 59. The top scorer was Neil Harris with 15 goals (in his first season in League football).

Wemberlee, Wemberlee, we're off to Wemberlee … the players are ecstatic after beating Walsall over two legs in the Southern Area final of the Auto Windscreens Shield.

Programme cover and ticket for the final at Wembley against Wigan, fifty-four years after The Lions' previous visit to the Twin Towers.

Millwall's Auto Windscreens Shield final team at Wembley on 18 April 1999. From left to right, back row: P. Ifill, R. Newman, T. Cahill, R. Sadlier, J. Dolan, S. Reid, J. Stuart. Front row: S. Nethercott, G. Lavin, N. Harris, mascot, B. Roberts. Millwall lost the game 0-1.

Millwall FC, 1999/2000. From left to right, back row: S. Reid, D. Hockton, S. Fitzgerald, S. Nethercott, J. Dolan, B. Law, L. Cort, P. Moody, R. Sadlier, S. Dyche, P. Ifill. Middle row: G. Docherty (physiotherapist), L. Odunsi, R. Ryan, K. Grant, L. Neill, P. Smith, N. Spink, N. Harris, A. Warner, R. Barnard, A. Cook, M. Bircham, R. Bowry, R. Newman, S. Gritt (coach). Front row: J. Carter, P. Shaw, T. Tyne, J. Stuart, R. Bull, A. McLeary (joint manager), K. Stevens (joint manager), T. Cahill, M. Gilkes, B. Bubb, M. Hicks, W. Mead. Millwall finished the season in fifth position, having won 23, drawn 13 and lost 10 games; they scored 76 goals and conceded 50. The top scorer was Neil Harris with 25 goals.

Millwall FC, 2000/2001. From left to right, back row: S. Reid, S. Fitzgerald, S. Nethercott, J. Dolan, P. Moody, R. Sadlier, L. Cort, D. Tuttle, S. Dyche, P. Ifill. Middle row: S. Gritt (coach), M. Bircham, A. Dunne, L. Neill, J. Stuart, M. Phillips, P. Smith, T. Warner, T. Tyne, N. Harris, D. Livermore, M. Lawrence, B. Bowry, G. Docherty (physiotherapist). Front row: R. Ryan, D. Meade, L. Odunsi, B. Bubb, C. Kinet, A. McLeary (joint manager), K. Stevens (joint manager), T. Cahill, R. Bull, M. Rees, M. Hicks, K. Braniff. Millwall finished the season as champions of Division Two, having won 28, drawn 9 and lost 9 matches; they scored 89 goals and conceded 38. The top scorer was Neil Harris with 27 goals.

Rhino and Macca were two of Millwall's most loyal servants, who between them chalked up over 900 appearances for the club in the various competitions. Keith Stevens was a product of the club's youth system and signed for The Lions as a professional in June 1981, two days after his seventeenth birthday. He had made his Football League debut in the last game of the 1980/81, when manager George Graham selected him for the match against Oxford United. Rhino was initially a right-back but, as his career progressed, was to play more as a (very consistent) centre-back. A serious injury in 1996 threatened his playing days and, although he did make a full recovery, his appearances for the first team were less frequent. He was handed the reserve team job at The Den and, when Billy Bonds was fired in May 1998, it was the opening Keith was looking for – later that month he was rewarded by being appointed first-team manager. With Alan McLeary installed as his assistant, Rhino led Millwall to their first visit to Wembley since 1945, when Millwall reached the final of the Auto Windscreens Trophy in 1999. Alan 'Macca' McLeary followed Rhino through the youth ranks at The Den, signing as a professional for the club in October 1984. Originally a midfield player, Alan was another convert to the back four – a role he filled quite admirably – and was to form a very effective partnership with Steve Wood during The Lion's promotion in 1988. When this continued during

Millwall's first season in the First Division, he was rewarded with selection (along with team-mate Terry Hurlock) to join the England 'B' squad tour during the summer of 1989. Macca suffered some loss of form after the Millwall's relegation in 1990 and moved on to Charlton Athletic in May 1993. After a eighteen month spell with Bristol City, Alan found himself in familiar surroundings in February 1997, when Lions boss John Docherty brought him back to The Den following Millwall's descent into administration. He became Rhino's assistant a year or so later, and then joint manager in May 1999. It appeared now that a stabilised Millwall were heading in the right direction, but a bombshell was to hit this part of London when, in early September 2000, both Keith Stevens and Alan McLeary were sacked. They were replaced by Mark McGhee; with the foundation laid by Rhino and Macca, he led The Lions to the First Division Championship in 2001.

Millwall players celebrating the news that they have been promoted after drawing 1-1 with Wrexham. Tim Cahill scored the equaliser that gave the Lions the point they needed after Reading lost at Colchester.

Champions! Millwall finished the 2000/01 season top of Division Two. The celebrations began after a 5-0 thrashing of Oldham; Paul Moody and Neil Harris got two apiece and Steven Reid a twenty-five yard scorcher. Matt Lawrence was given the Player of the Year award before the game, and then the home crowd of 18,510 watched from all four sides of the stadium as Millwall put on an impressive promotion show. Immediately after the match, Stuart Nethercott was presented with the Division Two trophy and the players are pictured here celebrating from the Nationwide rostrum – Division One here we come!